Mike McGrath

Access

In easy steps is an imprint of In Easy Steps Limited
16 Hamilton Terrace · Holly Walk · Leamington Spa
Warwickshire · United Kingdom · CV32 4LY
www.ineasysteps.com

Notice of Liability
Every effort has been made to ensure that this book contains accurate
and current information. However, In Easy Steps Limited and the
author shall not be liable for any loss or damage suffered by readers
as a result of any information contained herein.

Trademarks
Microsoft® and Windows® are registered trademarks of Microsoft
Corporation. All other trademarks are acknowledged as belonging to
their respective companies.

In Easy Steps Limited supports The Forest Stewardship Council (FSC),
the leading international forest certification organization. All our titles
that are printed on Greenpeace approved FSC certified paper carry the
FSC logo.

MIX
Paper from
responsible sources
FSC® C020837

Printed and bound in the United Kingdom

ISBN 978-1-84078-823-5

Contents

① Getting Started

Welcome to the exciting

world of databases with

Microsoft Access. This

chapter describes the

Access environment and

demonstrates the Access

user interface.

Introducing Access

Access is the latest version of Microsoft's popular Relational Database Management System (RDBMS). The Access application ("app") lets you manage all types of data with ease:

- Store and manipulate data in **Tables**

- Retrieve specific data by making **Queries**

- Provide user-friendly data entry **Forms**

- Supply attractively-styled data **Reports**

- Share data with colleagues using **Access**

Access is, however, much more than a means of storing and retrieving data. If you want to, you can build complete software apps limited only by your requirements and creativity.

You don't need to be a computer programmer to use Access as you can use nearly all of Access's functionality without entering a single line of code. All that is required is some forward planning and a clear idea of what purpose the database should serve.

What is a database?

A database is simply an ordered collection of records. For example, the Rolodex you may have on your office desk is a type of database. Open it up and you have the names, telephone numbers, and addresses of your business contacts.

In a computer, database information is organized in a much more structured way but the general idea is the same. Access keeps data in Tables. A Table is like the Rolodex – it contains all the data we need. Each row of the Table contains data about a specific thing. In a Rolodex it would be a business card. The columns of the Table help us to organize the data. Each column contains some specific item of data, such as the address of a contact.

The next chapter describes how databases are structured and demonstrates how to create them, but the rest of this chapter is devoted to getting you started with the Access app.

The New icon pictured above indicates new features of Access.

Start thinking about your database now. What do you want it to do? What information do you need to store in the database?

Launching the Access app

Access is typically launched by clicking the Access item on the Windows Start menu, to open the "Start" screen. Here you see a range of ready-made templates, and a list of recently-opened Access files that you can click to reopen:

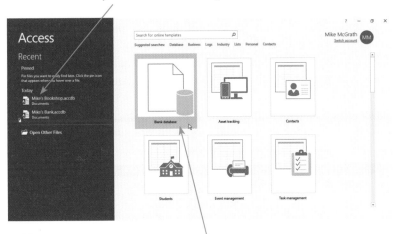

Hot tip

Access can also be launched by double-clicking on an existing database file icon. In that case, Access immediately opens that database in its user interface, by-passing this Start screen.

1 Click on the **Blank database** template icon to begin creating a brand new Access database

2 See a dialog box open that suggests a default name for the database and a default location on your computer

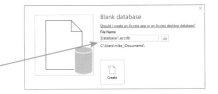

3 Accept the suggested defaults, or edit the dialog box to provide your preferred name and location – for example, rename the database as "FirstDatabase" and choose a **C:\MyDatabases** folder

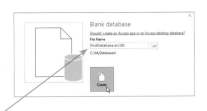

Hot tip

You may, optionally, omit the **.accdb** file extension when choosing a name – the file extension will be added automatically.

4 Click on the **Create** button to complete the creation of the new database at your chosen location – the database will now open in the Access user interface

9

Exploring the user interface

The Access user interface comprises several components that allow you to work efficiently with databases. In common with other apps in the Microsoft Office suite there is a "Ribbon" that intelligently groups related command icons on several menu tabs. Below the Ribbon is a Navigation Pane, containing icons that represent objects within the current database, and a Table window in which to view and edit the database content. Additionally, there is an editable Quick Access Toolbar for commands you frequently use, and a Status Bar that provides useful information:

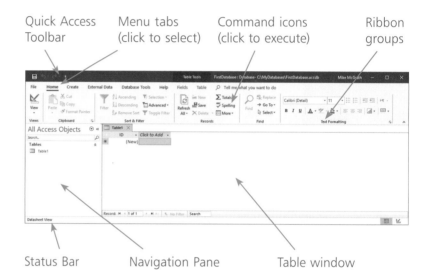

Quick Access Toolbar   Menu tabs (click to select)   Command icons (click to execute)   Ribbon groups

Status Bar   Navigation Pane   Table window

Hot tip

Press the **Alt** key to see keyboard shortcuts appear next to each Ribbon icon – press a shortcut key to activate the associated icon.

Hot tip

When you have a lot of windows open and space is at a premium you can close the Ribbon by double-clicking the tab that is currently selected – click any tab to reopen the Ribbon.

The Table window provides two possible views of the database:

● **Datasheet View** – displays the data within the database and allows you to enter and edit data, but does not allow you to change the format of the database.

● **Design View** – displays the format of the database and allows you to change the format of the database objects.

To choose the view of an opened Table:

1 Select the **Home** tab

2 Click the **View** icon in the "Views" group, then choose a view option – for example, choose Design View

3 See Design View open in the Table window and notice that the **Design** tab has become automatically selected

Hot tip

When first switching to Design View, a dialog may appear allowing you to choose a table name – you can use the suggested name ("Table1") or choose another name.

The Navigation Pane makes finding database objects such as Tables and Queries easier by filtering them according to their type, the date they were created, and their group:

1 At the top of the **Navigation Pane**, click the arrow button

2 From the drop-down menu that appears, select a category by clicking the category name once – such as "Filter By Group"

3 If any object groups exist, you can further refine your filter by clicking once on a group name

Navigation Pane with the **Queries** database object type filter applied

Hot tip

The Navigation Pane displays all the database objects – **Tables** that store data, **Queries** that search data, **Reports** that explain data, and **Forms** for data entry.

Don't forget

You will add database objects as you construct an Access database. Select any object in the **Navigation Pane** to open it in the Table window for modification.

Customizing Quick Access

The Quick Access Toolbar provides quick and convenient access to commonly-used commands such as Save, and is normally found at the top left of the Access screen.

By default, the Quick Access Toolbar features only three buttons – Save, Undo, and Redo. Although these are useful in themselves, the choice of action is somewhat limited. As your confidence with Access increases, you will soon want to have certain actions within easy reach. Happily, you can customize the Quick Access Toolbar, and add or delete extra buttons.

Customizing the Quick Access Toolbar

Buttons on the Quick Access Toolbar appear "grayed out" if that action is not available. Here, **Save** and **Undo** actions are available, but **Redo** is unavailable.

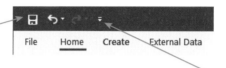

1 Click the arrow at the end of the Quick Access Toolbar – to open a drop-down menu

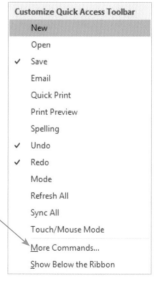

2 Click a menu item to add that command to the Quick Access Toolbar. Some of the most useful commands can be added to the Quick Access Toolbar using the drop-down menu, but many more commands are available

To add any action to the Quick Access Toolbar simply right-click it on the Ribbon and select the **Customize Quick Access Toolbar** option.

3 Click the **More Commands...** menu item – to open the "Access Options" dialog, shown opposite

Select the
action to
add here

Click here to
see different
groups of
actions

Click here
to add the
selected action

Change the
order in which
actions are
displayed on
the Toolbar

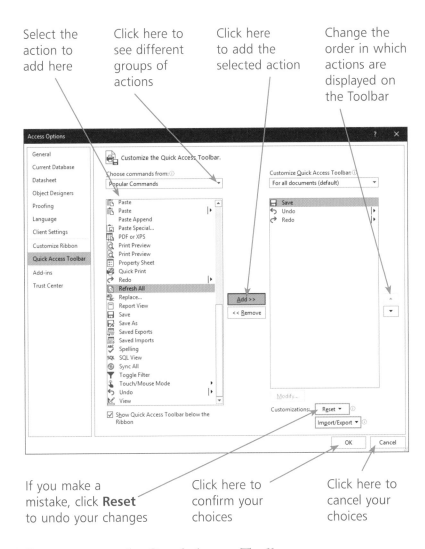

Hot tip

It's often convenient
to distinguish between
different groups of
actions according to
their function, for
example separating file
access actions from Table
creation actions. In order
to separate actions on
the Quick Access Toolbar,
choose the **Separator**
action.

If you make a
mistake, click **Reset**
to undo your changes

Click here to
confirm your
choices

Click here to
cancel your
choices

Repositioning the Quick Access Toolbar

1 Click the arrow at the end of the Quick Access Toolbar

2 Click the **Show Below the Ribbon** menu option to
position the Quick Access Toolbar below the Ribbon

Don't forget

To return the Quick
Access Toolbar to its
default position, click the
arrow button, then click
the **Show Above the
Ribbon** menu option.

Managing files Backstage

The File button on the Access menu opens the "Backstage" screen where you can perform both file management and database administration tasks. The Backstage screen allows you to Open, Save, and perform maintenance operations on your database.

Hot tip

To open the Backstage screen quickly, press the **Alt** + **F** keys.

Opening a database

1 Click the **File** menu button

2 Click **Open** from the Backstage menu

3 Select **Recent**, **OneDrive**, or **This PC** to choose the database location – for example, select **This PC**

4 Select the folder containing the database – for example, select a folder at **C:\MyDatabases** on your computer

5 Double-click the database file icon to open that database

Hot tip

You can click on the Folders item to navigate to other folders.

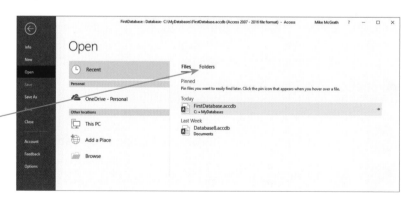

By default, Access opens a database in a restricted mode of operation. Specifically, it disables the execution of "Visual Basic for Applications" (VBA) code and Macros. To enable all the features of the database, click the Enable Content button on the "Security Warning" that appears between the Ribbon and the main database window, or click the link to see more information:

Beware

Only enable content if you are absolutely certain that it doesn't contain malicious code. In most cases, such code would only be present if you were opening a database from someone else.

This opens the Backstage screen, where you can discover what content has been disabled. Click the Enable Content button then choose the Enable All Content option to enable all the features of the database, or choose Advanced Options to enable only specific features of the database.

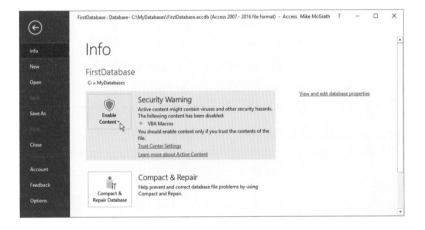

Saving a database

1 Click the **Save** button on the Quick Access Toolbar

2 Or, click the **File** button to open Backstage, then click the **Save** option

Hot tip

To save a database quickly at any point, press the **Ctrl + S** keys.

...cont'd

Beware

By default, Access suggests the name "Database" followed by a number – for example, "Database1". Avoid naming your databases in this manner, as having similarly-named databases can be confusing and may cause errors.

Creating a new database

1 Click the **File** button to open Backstage

2 Click the **New** menu option

3 Click the **Blank database** icon

4 Enter a name for your new database in the dialog, and choose a location at which to save the database on your computer

5 Press the **Create** button

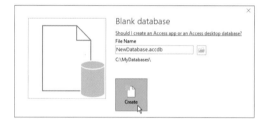

Closing a database and exiting Access

Although Access is a great app, there will come a time when you want to close a database and switch off Access:

1 Click the **File** button to open Backstage

2 Click the **Close** menu option – to close the currently-open database

3 Click the **X** button at the top right of the Access window, or press the **Alt** + **F4** keys

Personalizing Access options

The "Access Options" dialog contains various settings that affect the way you view and interact with Access. For example, you can decide whether or not you want feature descriptions to appear in the Screen Tips such as the one below, which appears when you place your cursor over the Table icon on the Create menu:

Table

Create a new blank table. You can define the fields directly in the new table, or open the table in Design view.

❓ **Tell me more**

① Click on the **File** button to open Backstage

② Click on the **Options** menu item, located at the bottom of the Backstage menu

③ Click the menu items at the left-hand side of the "Access Options" dialog to switch between sets of options

④ Click on the drop-down menus to change option settings

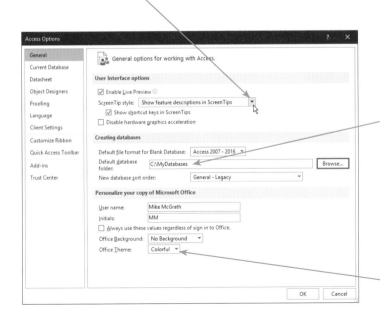

Notice that you can specify a default database folder of your choice in this example.

Access has introduced the option to have **Colorful, Dark Gray, Black**, or **White** themes.

Converting older databases

Access makes it easy to open and work with a database created with an older version of Access, such as those in the MDB (**.mdb**) file format used by Access 2003. The older database will look and feel exactly the same as a database created with later versions of Access – but you won't be able to make use of the newer features available in modern Access. Luckily, Access can quickly convert your old database to the newer ACCDB (**.accdb**) file format so that you can use the newer features in modern Access:

Although it's always a great idea to back up files, it is not necessary to backup an Access database when converting to other file formats, as Access generates a new COPY of the current database. It does not replace the current file. This means that converting in either direction leaves you with both an ACCDB file and an MDB file.

1 Open the database you want to convert in modern Access, then click the **File** button to open Backstage

2 Click the **Save As** menu option

3 Choose **Save Database As** under the "File Types" heading

4 Double-click **Access Database (*.accdb)** under the "Save Database As" heading – to open a "Save As" dialog

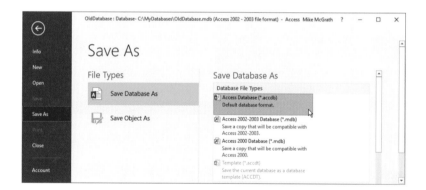

Beware

After you've converted a database to the newer ACCDB file format you will no longer be able to use it with the earlier version of Access.

5 Choose a location, then click the **Save** button to create a converted copy of the old-format database

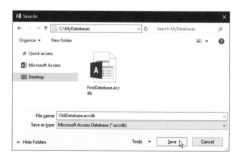

By default, a converted database retains the original name but gets the different file extension.

6 Click the **OK** button to dismiss the warning dialog

...cont'd

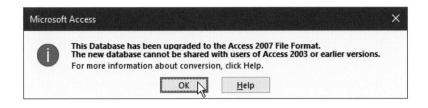

The ACCDB file format was introduced in Access 2007. So that year is shown when converting from the old MDB format.

Converting databases to older formats

You may sometimes need to convert your modern Access database to a file format that will work with previous versions of Access:

1 Open the database you want to convert in modern Access, then click the **File** button to open Backstage

2 Click the **Save As** menu option, then choose **Save Database As** under the "File Types" heading

3 Double-click **Access 2002-2003 Database (*.mdb)** under "Save Database As" – to open a "Save As" dialog

Consider your options carefully before you convert a database to an older file format, as you will no longer be able to use the new features of modern Access.

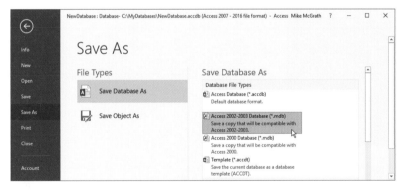

4 Choose a location, then click the **Save** button to create a converted copy of the new-format database

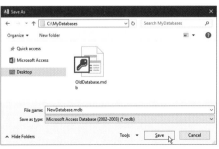

Templates are downloaded from an online repository so you will need to have an internet connection to open templates that are not already on your computer.

Scroll through the list of popular templates to discover some great ideas on how you might use the Access app.

Using Access templates

Access provides many high-quality templates that, for most people, can be used straight out of the box. For example, if your sole reason for investing in a Relational Database Management System is to maintain the contact details of your customers, then the Access "Contacts" template might be perfect for your needs.

The best way to see if Access templates are right for your organization is to open them up and see what they do:

Opening a template

1 Launch Access from the Windows Start menu to see the Access Start screen – or close all open databases, then click the **File** button to see the Access templates

2 From the scrollable list of popular templates on the Start screen, click on the **Contacts** template

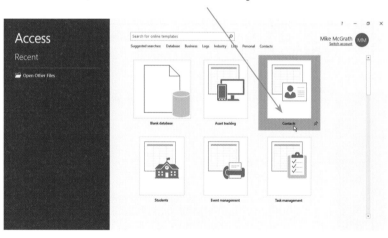

3 Enter a name and location in the dialog, then click the **Create** button to create a database from the template

4 You will now see a **Welcome** screen appear that provides a brief description of the database and offers assistance

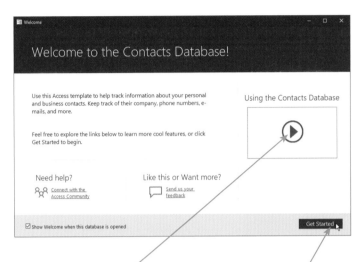

You will need to have an internet connection to watch the online video.

5 Click the arrow button to watch an online video demonstrating how to use this database

6 Click the **Get Started** button to open the database in your Access app

7 Make all features available so you can begin to use this database by clicking the **Enable Content** button

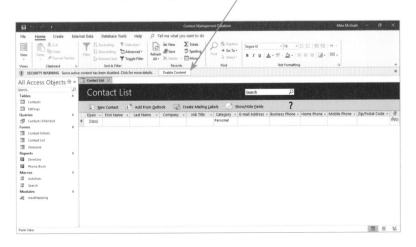

You can safely **Enable Content** when using Microsoft Office templates to enable their Macro code functions.

Searching for templates

If you're looking for a template to use in Access, but you can't instantly see an appropriate template in the list of popular templates on the Start screen, you can easily search the thousands of Microsoft Office online templates to find something suitable. For example, you might want to create a database to retain important details of personal belongings for insurance purposes:

Beware

The search will return templates for use with all Microsoft Office apps, including Word, Excel, and PowerPoint – not all results can be used as templates for Access databases.

22

1 Launch Access from the Windows Start menu to see the Access Start screen – or close all open databases, then click the **File** button to see the templates

2 Next, type "personal belongings" into the Search box at the top of the Start screen

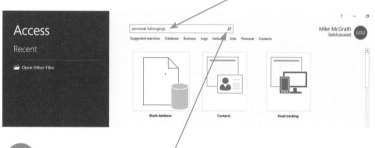

3 Now, click the Search button, or hit the **Enter** key, to perform a search for a suitable template

Don't forget

Simply click on the template icon in the search result to download and use that template in Access.

4 The search finds a suitable "Home Inventory" template, and the result indicates the categories in which this template can be found

As an alternative to searching by typing text into the Start screen's Search box, you can also search categories for a suitable template. Links to popular categories appear as hyperlinks below the Search box. To find a template for a database of personal belongings, it is reasonable to explore the "Personal" and "Inventories" categories:

1 Open the Access Start screen, then click the **Personal** hyperlink to explore that category

The items that appear as "Suggested searches" may vary according to your previous template search history.

2 The suitable "Home Inventory" template is found alongside other templates in the **Personal** category

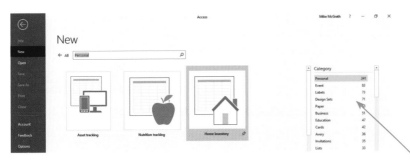

23

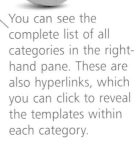

3 Return to the Access Start screen, then click the **Inventories** hyperlink to explore that category

4 The suitable "Home Inventory" template is found alongside other templates in the **Inventories** category

You can see the complete list of all categories in the right-hand pane. These are also hyperlinks, which you can click to reveal the templates within each category.

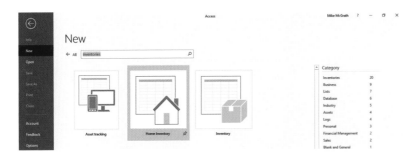

Getting some Help

If you need assistance at any time in the Access app, you can call upon the Access Help feature:

1 Open any database in Access, then simply press the **F1** key (or press **Fn + F1** keys) to see a Help window appear in the Access app

2 You can click on any item you want to get help with. For example, if you are looking for help when you're new to Access, click the **Get started** item

3 Click the **Play** button to watch a video introducing the Access app

4 Click the arrow beside the Search box to return to the Help window

5 Choose another item, such as **Tables**, to see a list of topics

6 Select a topic from the list, such as **Introduction to tables**, to see more

7 Now select a sub-topic, such as **Overview**, for help

24

You can search for assistance in a **Help** window:

1 Enter keywords for a subject, such as "keyboard shortcuts"

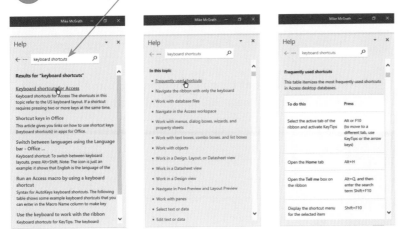

Whichever topic you select, you will still have the **Search** box so you can locate new topics, or click the **X** button on the Help window to close it.

2 Click on any result topic – such as **Frequently used shortcuts** – for help on that specific subject

You can also seek assistance by typing a query word or phrase into the **Tell me what you want to do** box on the Access title bar:

1 Enter "keyboard shortcuts" into the **Tell Me** box

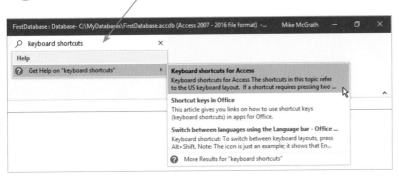

The **Tell Me** box is a great feature in modern Access. Type in anything you like, and Access will attempt to help you.

2 Click the arrow button on the context menu that appears – to reveal a list of suggested options

3 Select the **Keyboard shortcuts for Access** option to open the Help window for that topic, as shown above center

Applying Access updates

Microsoft will, by default, automatically update Access with new features as they become available. If you prefer not to enable automatic updates for the Access app, you can manually check for and apply updates at any time:

1 In Access, click the **File** button to open Backstage

2 Click the **Account** menu option to see your Microsoft Office **User Information** and **Product Information**

You can also change the **Office Background** and **Office Theme** settings to your preference using the drop-down menus on the Account screen.

3 Click the **Office Updates, Update Options** button to open a menu offering various settings options

4 Choose the **Update Now** option to apply all available updates immediately

Choose the **View Updates** option to discover which new features have been recently installed.

5 Choose the **Disable Updates** option to stop receiving automatic updates

When you revisit these update options you will see an Enable Updates option that you can choose to resume automatic updates.

2 Designing Databases

This chapter describes database relationships and explains the benefits of good database design.

Arranging related data

For maximum efficiency, databases store their data in related tables that contain records and fields.

Data

The term "data" refers to the information stored within a database. The data is best broken into individual items for greater flexibility. For example, names such as "John Smith" are best broken into forename "John" and surname "Smith", so a collection of names could be sorted by first name or be sorted by last name.

Tables

A "Table" is the format in which a database stores items of data. For example, a transactions Table with columns for number, date, amount, and client stores each transaction on a separate row:

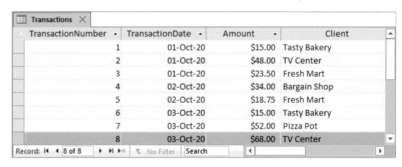

TransactionNumber	TransactionDate	Amount	Client
1	01-Oct-20	$15.00	Tasty Bakery
2	01-Oct-20	$48.00	TV Center
3	01-Oct-20	$23.50	Fresh Mart
4	02-Oct-20	$34.00	Bargain Shop
5	02-Oct-20	$18.75	Fresh Mart
6	03-Oct-20	$15.00	Tasty Bakery
7	03-Oct-20	$52.00	Pizza Pot
8	03-Oct-20	$68.00	TV Center

Relationships

A "relational" database is a collection of Tables containing data, which are related to each other through common items. For example, a Table of clients, storing name and address data, could be related to the Table above by the "Client" column item. This provides maximum flexibility and is the most efficient database design. An Access database must contain at least two Tables to be considered relational.

To be used most effectively an Access database will, therefore, contain more than one Table. In a relational database a Table is based upon a particular concept or entity, typically something concrete such as a car, and holds data specific to that particular entity. For example, in a bank database you might have a customer Table that holds data about the customers of that bank, such as their names, their sex, and the amount of cash they have invested with the bank.

Hot tip

Data stored in a single Table format is known as a "flat-file system", such as an Excel spreadsheet. Relational databases are better at avoiding duplication for accounting, inventory, and invoicing purposes.

Another Table you might see in a bank database is an account Table, which describes the type of account a particular customer holds as well as the current balance. A Table consists of a number of columns, more formally known as "fields", and a number of rows, more formally known as "records". Logical links between Tables are called relationships.

Fields

A "field" is the technical name for a database Table column and is used to denote a specific type of data. For example, in a car Table you might have a color field denoting the color of a car. The "Sex" field (column) below contains text data denoting customer gender:

Sex ▾
Male
Male
Female
Male
Female
Male

Each field in a Table holds only one type of data; for example, text data describing gender.

Records

A "record" is the technical name for a database Table row and contains the actual data in a Table. Whereas a field describes the type of data in a Table, such as customer gender, a record denotes whether a particular customer is male or female. If you think of a Table as a description of an object, such as a car, then the records (rows) of a Table represent the actual cars:

CarNumber ▾	Model ▾	EngineSize ▾	Transmission
1	Highlander	4.0	Auto
2	Highlander	3.0	Auto
3	Costa	1.4	Manual
4	CostaSport	2.0	Manual
5	Siesta	1.0	Auto

Record: I ◂ 5 of 5 ▸ ▸I ▸✱ ✕ No Filter Search

Each record in a Table contains the same fields but (usually) has different data in those fields.

Although it's tempting to refer to a field as a column, and a record as a row, this can cause confusion between fields and other objects. This book generally refers to data in a Table column as a field, and data in a Table row as a record.

Understanding relationships

A relational database simply wouldn't be relational without relationships – but what exactly are these relationships? And why are they so important? A relationship is a logical connection between one Table and another. The connection is made between a field in one Table and a field in another Table. For example, below are two Tables – a branch Table and an account Table:

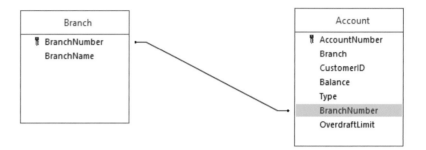

One branch of a bank will contain many customer accounts. By relating the BranchNumber field of the Branch Table to the BranchNumber field in the Accounts Table, you are creating a "One-to-Many" relationship between the two Tables. There are three different types of relationship you can define between Tables – One-to-Many, One-to-One, and Many-to-Many:

One-to-Many
A One-to-Many relationship occurs when one Table, known as the "parent" Table, has many matching records in another Table, known as the "child" Table. In the example above, the "Branch" parent has many matching records in the "Account" child Table.

One-to-One
A One-to-One relationship occurs when there is a direct match between a record in one Table and a record in another. For example, at the top of the next page are two Tables – a customer Table and an address Table. The business logic behind the relationship states that a customer may only have one address at any one time. Every one record in the "Customer" Table therefore directly matches one record in the "Address" Table.

One-to-Many relationships link ONE record in the first Table to MANY records in the second Table – this is the most common Table relationship.

One-to-One relationships link ONE record in the first Table to exactly ONE record in the second Table.

30

Many-to-Many

A Many-to-Many relationship occurs when one Table can have many possible matches with records of another Table, and vice versa. To model this relationship in Access, you must create a third Table, known as a "Junction" Table, and reduce the Many-to-Many relationship between two Tables into two One-to-Many relationships – using the Junction Table as the intermediary:

Many-to-Many relationships link MANY records in the first Table to MANY records in the second Table.

31

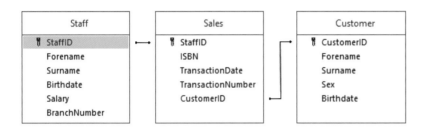

Relationships in a typical database might look like this:

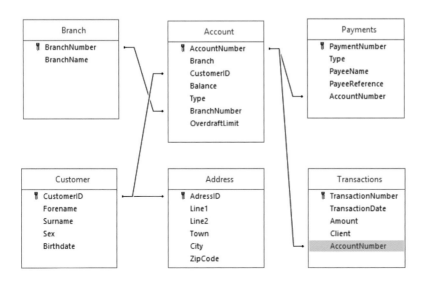

A Junction Table keeps track of related records in two other Tables.

Developing database design

Good database design is essential for creating a database that stores and retrieves information accurately and efficiently. Fortunately, the basic principles of database design are easy to learn and apply to your own databases. It is, however, important to recognize and apply these principles to achieve the best results.

The benefits of good database design

There are many reasons why spending a little time on the careful planning and preparation of your new database is a good idea. Not only will it help focus your mind on the problem you're trying to solve, it will also reduce the number of errors in your database that will need correcting later. It is useful to sketch your design on paper to visualize your database design requirements.

Good database design can provide these benefits:

- **Remove** duplicated or unnecessary data.

- **Reduce** the size of the database file.

- **Increase** the efficiency of the database.

- **Maintain** the accuracy of data within the database.

The trouble with redundant data

"Redundant data" is either data that is repeated in another Table or data that could be calculated by Access, so it doesn't have to be stored at all. For example, a Table may have a field for a customer's date of birth and their age. In this case, the age field is unnecessary as the age can be calculated by subtracting the customer's date of birth from today's date. Redundant data increases the database file size unnecessarily. This may seem unimportant when you only have a small amount of data in your database, but as the amount of data stored in your database increases, so will the length of time it takes Access to perform a Query or produce a Report. In designing a database, redundant data is, therefore, something to be avoided at all costs!

Write a list of every possible piece of information your database will need to store to discover the required fields.

A well-designed relational database will use as little storage as possible by eliminating duplicated and redundant data.

Riding the Development Life Cycle

Every project needs a plan, and the creation of an Access database is no exception. Database developers use the "Development Life Cycle" as their guide when planning a database. The Development Life Cycle flows from top to bottom:

- **Discover** the field requirements.

- **Design** the database Tables.

- **Create** the database records.

- **Produce** Forms, Queries, and Reports.

- **Test** the database thoroughly.

The first three stages of the Development Life Cycle have the most bearing on the accuracy and effectiveness of your database design. As you progress through this book you will develop your own ideas about the way your Forms should work, what Queries need to be performed, and what Reports are required to produce.

Meeting the requirements

The first thing to do is to find out what the requirements are, which simply means asking the question: "What precisely do you want the database to do?" It might sound an obvious question, but many computing projects have failed because the designers didn't know precisely what they should be creating.

Before you begin designing your database, question the people who will ultimately use it to find out exactly what they expect of it. Find out what Queries they'll need to make and what Reports they'll need to print.

You are trying to discover the user requirements – the exact needs of the end users. Note down their responses and keep an organized record of what the finished database should do. As you work through the different stages of the Development Life Cycle, refer back to these requirements to make sure you're still on the right track.

Forms allow users to enter data into the database; Queries retrieve specific data from the database; and Reports present selected data from the database.

"Plan Your Work"
then
"Work Your Plan".

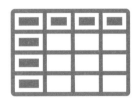

Producing data Tables

Tables as entities

What you're aiming to do when designing a database is to take a good, hard look at some aspect of real life and model it in a way that's compatible with Access. For example, a design for a bookshop database might model real-life entities such as customers and shop assistants, and the transactions that occur between them such as buying a book or making a refund.

A good way to visualize this is to imagine watching a film about the bit of real life you want to store data about, such as a bookshop, and then pausing it. Think about the actors in the scene and the data we might want to store about them.

A customer has a name and an address so you would want to keep that information in your database – you could use that to keep the customer informed of special offers and the latest stock titles. Similarly, you would need to keep the same data on a shop assistant so that you could mail their pay check to them.

You would also want to store information about the books on sale, such as the title, author, and price:

BookID	Title	Author	Price
1	Camino Island	John Grisham	$19.95
2	Wired	Julie Garwood	$17.50
3	Dangerous	Milo Yiannopoulos	$18.00
4	Use of Force	Brad Thor	$16.75
5	The Woman in Cabin 10	Ruth Ware	$18.25
6	The Identicals	Elin Hilderbrand	$16.80
7	Murder Games	James Patterson	$16.75
8	Rediscovering Americanism	Mark R. Levin	$16.20
9	The Handmaid's Tale	Margaret Atwood	$14.70
10	The Stolen Girls	Patricia Gibney	$11.65

Imagine the scene you wish to model, and jot down the names of the actors and objects that appear in it.

The name of your Table will be the name of the entity you are modeling; "Customer", for example. Data about the entity, such as "Name" or "Sex", will be the fields of your Table.

Hot tip

Tables are often based on real-life objects or concepts so the name of a **Table** should always be noun-based, such as "Customer" or "Books".

Choosing Primary Keys and Foreign Keys

Tables are related to each other by common fields, as described on page 30, but how do you choose these fields?

Every Table must have a field that uniquely identifies individual records. For example, if you wanted to identify each record in a "Cars" Table uniquely you could use a field called "Vehicle Identification Number", or "VIN" – as a car's VIN is something that uniquely identifies it. Similarly, if you wanted to identify each record in an "Employee" Table you could use a field called "Payroll Number" – as an employee's payroll number is something that uniquely identifies that person within a company.

A field that uniquely identifies individual records is called a "Primary Key". Examine the fields you've chosen for your Tables to determine which field could become the Primary Key. There must only be one field that could possibly be a Primary Key within a Table. If you have more than one field that could be a Primary Key, you probably need to split the Table into two or more Tables.

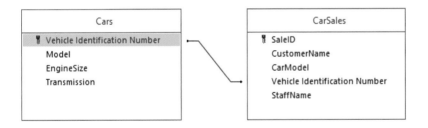

When you relate two Tables you are making a link between a Primary Key and a "Foreign Key". A Foreign Key is the field in a Table that exactly matches the Primary Key field of another Table. For example, to relate the "Cars" Table with another Table called "CarSales", containing records of all cars sold in a particular dealership, then you could include a "Vehicle Identification Number" field in the "CarSales" Table as the Foreign Key. By relating the two "Vehicle Identification Number" fields you are linking the information in both Tables in a logical manner.

No value in a Primary Key field can be **null** (that is, empty). Something has to be entered into it.

It is possible to have a Primary Key consisting of two or more fields that, when combined together, uniquely identify individual records in a Table. However, this is not a good idea and should be avoided. The only exception to this rule is when you need to create a **Junction Table** to model a Many-to-Many relationship.

A **Foreign Key** in another Table doesn't have to have the same name as the Primary Key to which it relates.

35

Optimizing database design

Normalization
The final part of database Table design is called "normalization". This is the process of gradually refining Tables to protect the integrity and accuracy of the data stored within them. This also helps save disk space by reducing the likelihood of redundant data. Normalization involves restructuring Tables into the First, then the Second, and then the Third "Normal Form".

First Normal Form (1NF)
Firstly, a field should only contain one value. For example, an address should be broken up into individual fields. You shouldn't put a whole address into one field.

Second Normal Form (2NF)
Secondly, every field in the Table should be fully dependent on the Primary Key. For example, in an "Employee" Table with "Payroll Number" as the Primary Key and two fields called "Name" and "Department", the Name field is fully dependent on Payroll Number because the two are intrinsically linked to each other, but the Department field isn't – an employee could work in any department but will only ever have one Payroll number.

Third Normal Form (3NF)
Thirdly, non-Primary Key fields should not be dependent on other non-Primary Key fields.

Defining business rules
Deciding which Tables to include in your database and how they are related to each other is only one part of the design. In order to model more closely the real-life scenarios of a business, you need to consider the business rules that govern it. Business rules, or business logic, are those often-unwritten and unacknowledged codes of conduct that you follow at work every day. No one considers them except when designing databases because they are usually a matter of common sense. For example, a business rule for a bank would be "Overdraft limits must be $0.00 or less". Write down the business rules that are relevant for your database so you can implement and enforce them as you progress.

If the database you are designing is not mission-critical or doesn't contain vast numbers of Tables, it is not strictly necessary to normalize the Tables past First Normal Form – but it is a good idea to do so.

If Tables do not satisfy Second and Third Normal Forms then they must be split into two or more Tables that do satisfy normalization.

The "Analyze" group on the Access **Database Tools** tab provides an **Analyze Performance** tool that you can use to examine the database design, and a **Database Documenter** tool that you can use to produce a printable summary of the database design.

3 Creating Tables

This chapter describes how to create database Tables, and demonstrates how to store data in fields and records.

Exploring the Table window

The Table window is the essential part of the Access interface in which you can create and edit your database Tables. You can add or remove fields and records, or modify data content, and easily switch between multiple Tables:

Components of the Table window

Hot tip

Change how you view a Table by right-clicking the tab of a Table and choosing **Design View** or **Datasheet View** from the context menu.

Hot tip

Close all Tables quickly by right-clicking the tab of any Table and choosing **Close All** from the context menu.

Click the tabs to switch between Tables

Select a field by clicking on its heading

Click to close the currently-selected Table

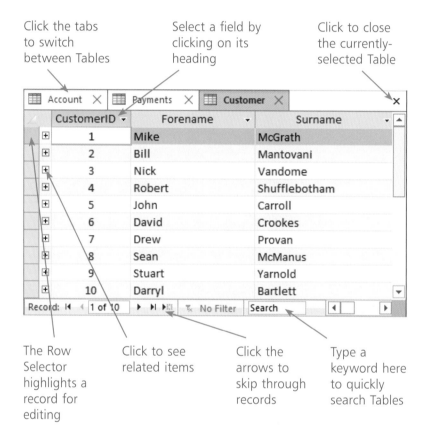

The Row Selector highlights a record for editing

Click to see related items

Click the arrows to skip through records

Type a keyword here to quickly search Tables

Switching between Views

1 **Open any Table** in Access

2 Click the **View** icon in the "Views" group on the **Home** tab, then select Datasheet View or Design View

Hot tip

Save a Table by clicking the **Save** icon on the Quick Access Toolbar.

Using Table templates

Although databases are designed for different purposes, much of the data kept in them is similar. For example, most businesses want to know the contact details of their customers. "Quick Start" templates exploit this commonality by providing ready-made Table templates that contain all fields that most organizations will want to include in their databases. Furthermore, a Table created using a template can be altered to suit your exact requirements:

1 Open a database in Access

2 Click the **Application Parts** icon in the "Templates" group on the Ribbon's **Create** tab

3 Click the **Contacts** icon in the Quick Start menu – to open a "Create Relationship" dialog

4 Check the dialog's "There is no relationship" option, then click its **Create** button

Once you've selected a **Table** template you can change it at any time. Customize it by adding or deleting fields, setting input masks, or specifying particular formats for data types.

39

5 Click the **Contacts** Table that gets added to the Navigation Pane to see the ready-made Table appear

6 Other related Contacts templates have also been added to the database. Unless you want these too, hold down the **Shift** key and click each template to select them, then right-click on them and choose **Delete** from the context menu

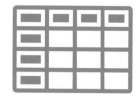

Working in Datasheet View

Datasheet View is the default data entry view for Access. Using the Datasheet View to build and manage your Tables couldn't be simpler:

Creating a Table in Datasheet View

1 Click the **Create** tab on the Ribbon

2 Click the **Table** icon located in the "Tables" group

3 Press the 🖫 **Save** icon on the Quick Access Toolbar

4 Enter the name of your new Table into the "Save As" dialog that now appears

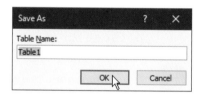

5 Click the **OK** button to create a Table

Access automatically creates a field called "ID", which can be renamed or deleted to suit your requirements, and provides a "Click to Add" heading that is prompting you to add fields.

Before you can save a **Table** it must first contain at least one field.

Adding fields in Datasheet View

Access provides two methods for adding fields to a Table. The first method is available within the Table window:

1 Click the **Click to Add** field heading

2 Select a data type for that field from the drop-down list that appears. For example, choose the **Number** data type

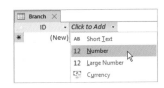

3 Type a field heading title – to replace the default heading

The second method is available within the Access Ribbon:

1 Click the **Fields** tab on the Ribbon

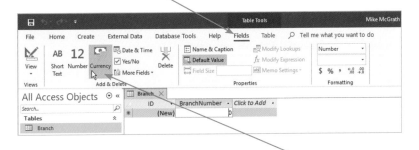

2 Select a data type for that field from the "Add & Delete" group. For example, choose the **Currency** data type

3 Type a field heading title – to replace the default heading

To move a field after it's been created, highlight it by clicking once on its heading. Then, click and hold the left mouse button on the field heading again. A black stripe should appear along the left side of the field. Still holding the mouse button, move the black stripe to the required position then let go of the mouse button.

To resize field width, position the mouse cursor between two headings to see the cursor change, then click and drag the field border.

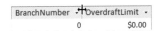

Formatting Datasheets

Renaming fields in Datasheet View

There are times when it is necessary to rename a field that already exists. For example, you might need to rename a field because a field in another related Table already has that name:

You should always give your fields meaningful names so you know what data they are supposed to represent. For example, if a field holds data about a car's color then name it "Car Color" and not "Field 2".

1 Click the heading of the field you want to rename

2 Click the **Fields** tab on the Ribbon

3 Next, open the "Enter Field Properties" dialog by clicking the **Name & Caption** icon in the "Properties" group

4 Type a new heading in the "Name" input box, then click the **OK** button to apply the change

Deleting fields in Datasheet View

If you delete a field, you cannot **Undo** the action to return the deleted field to the Table.

1 Click the heading of the field you want to delete

2 Click the **Fields** tab on the Ribbon

3 Click the **Delete** icon in the "Add & Delete" group

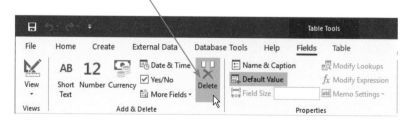

Specifying a data type in Datasheet View

In Datasheet View, choosing a data type for your field is a matter of point-and-click simplicity. A full discussion of Access data types appears later in this chapter, but essentially a data type dictates the type of data that can be entered into a field. For example, if you assign the Number data type to a field then only digits can be entered into it. Typing a letter into it will generate an error message. Using a Number data type would therefore make it impossible to enter text into a field intended to hold quantity or bank account numbers:

Click here to change the data type

Checking this box forces users to enter a value

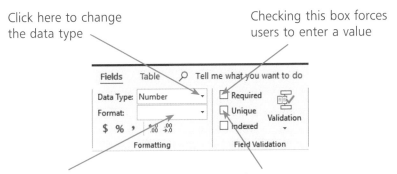

Click here to change the way data within the field is displayed

Check this box to ensure that every value in the field is different

A data type gives meaning to the data in your Tables. It also helps to validate the data entered into a field.

43

Formatting Number and Currency data types

The data type options in the "Formatting" group make it quick and easy to apply specific formatting to Currency and Number formats. To apply a format, simply click a value within that field to highlight it, then click the formatting icon relevant to your needs:

Applies Currency format

Inserts a comma after each thousand

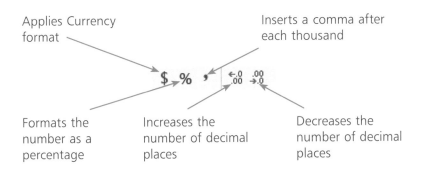

Formats the number as a percentage

Increases the number of decimal places

Decreases the number of decimal places

Working in Design View

Although it is easy to create Tables in Datasheet View, it isn't the most efficient way of building Tables. The alternative Design View is faster and gives a greater degree of control over the properties of your fields.

The Design View screen gives you a clear view of the fields that make up your Table, and the properties and constraints you have placed on each field.

Always try to use Design View when you first create your Tables, only using Datasheet View to fine-tune your Tables as you work with live data.

The Design View screen

Hot tip

Keep field names short and avoid using spaces as you will need to type these when referring to them in **Queries**, **Forms**, and **Reports**. Use only letters, numbers, and the underscore character.

44

Type field names in this column

Choose data types from the drop-down menu

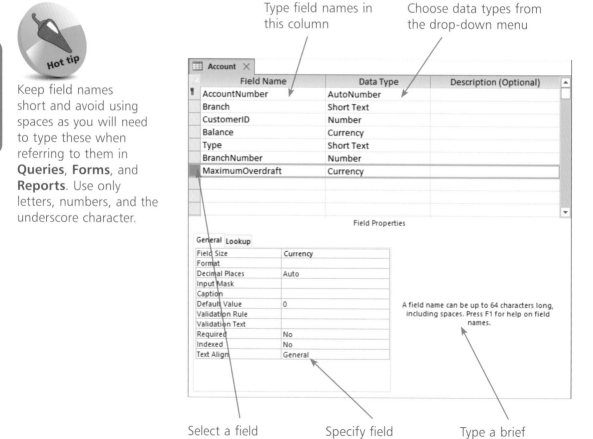

Select a field by clicking the Row Selector

Specify field properties within this pane

Type a brief description of your field in this column

Creating a Table

Design View contains everything you need to create a perfect
Table design for all the fields you need:

1 Click the **Create** tab on the Ribbon

2 Click the **Table Design** icon in the "Tables" group – to
see a new empty Table open in Design View

3 Type a title for the **Field Name**

4 Press the Tab key to move to the
Data Type column

5 Choose a data type from the drop-
down menu; for example, **Number**

6 Press the Tab key to move to the
Description column

7 Type a brief description of the field

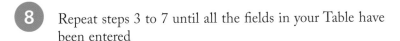

8 Repeat steps 3 to 7 until all the fields in your Table have
been entered

9 Click the **Save** icon on the Quick Access Toolbar

10 Enter the name of your new Table into the "Save As"
dialog, then click the **OK** button to save your design

Hot tip

Get into the habit of
always entering the
Primary Key for the
Table first – so you
always know that the
first field in the Design
View screen is the
Primary Key.

45

Managing rows

Access provides two methods for inserting and deleting Table rows in Design View:

Context menu

1 Right-click on a row to select it and open a context menu

2 Click the **Insert Rows** item on the context menu – to insert a row above the currently-selected row

You can use the **Undo** button on the Quick Access Toolbar to remove a newly-added row.

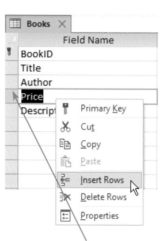

3 Right-click a row to select it and open a context menu, then click the **Delete Rows** menu item to delete that row

The Ribbon

1 Click a row, then select the **Design** tab on the Ribbon

2 Click the **Insert Rows** icon or **Delete Rows** icon in the "Tools" group – to add or remove a row

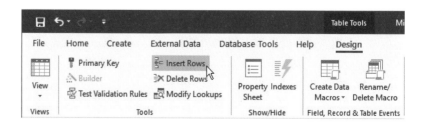

Setting the Primary Key

The Primary Key is a special field that is used to make relationships between Tables. The value in a Primary Key field uniquely identifies the rest of the data in that field. For example, the "Books" Table below uses the "ISBN" Number field as the Primary Key because it uniquely identifies a book. In the Access app, setting the Primary Key is simple:

1 Click the **Home** tab on the Ribbon

2 Click the **View** icon in the "Views" group, then select **Design View** – to switch to Design View

3 Click on the field to be made a **Primary Key** to select it

Books	
Field Name	**Data Type**
ISBN	Number
Title	Short Text
Author	Short Text
Price	Currency
Description	Long Text

4 Select the **Design** tab, then click the **Primary Key** icon in the "Tools" group

5 See a key icon now appear in the **Row Selector** to denote that this field is set as the Primary Key of the Table

Books	
Field Name	**Data Type**
ISBN	Number
Title	Short Text
Author	Short Text
Price	Currency
Description	Long Text

Hot tip

Alternatively, you can right-click a field name and select the **Primary Key** option from the context menu that appears.

Hot tip

Delete a Primary Key by right-clicking the key icon and selecting the **Primary Key** option from the context menu.

Don't forget

It's possible to use more than one field as the Primary Key. To add another Primary Key, hold down the **Ctrl** key while following the steps detailed here.

Selecting data types

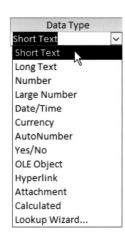

Using the correct data types will help others make sense of your database, and will help to prevent errors. The data type you choose for a field depends on the context and purpose of that field within your database. For example, if you want to record the date and time of a purchase then the Date/Time data type should be used. Below are listed brief descriptions of the data types available in Access:

Short Text

Can contain up to 255 characters of letters and numbers (alphanumeric data) – useful for names, addresses, titles, phone numbers, etc.

Long Text

Can contain up to 65,535 characters of letters and numbers (alphanumeric data) – useful for sentences and paragraphs. Rich Text Formatting can be applied to data in a Long Text field to add a bit of color.

Number

Can contain only numeric data – useful for quantities and ages. You can specify whether a field should use decimal places and, if so, how many places are allowed. You can also format values as percentages, such as 20%, or in scientific notation, such as 2.00E+01.

Large Number

Can contain only numeric data for very large numbers – useful for efficient calculations involving very large numbers.

Date/Time

Can contain dates in a variety of formats, regardless of how the user entered them. Access will automatically alter the date entered to suit the format that has been specified. Time can be viewed in 24-hour and 12-hour formats.

The **Large Number** data type was introduced in modern Access to support calculations with very large numbers.

Hot tip

Users now have the option of using a calendar to input dates. To use it, click a cell in a **Date/Time** field and click the ▦ calendar icon that appears at the right-hand side.

Currency

Can contain monetary numeric data. Calculations can be performed on the data stored within the Currency data type, and values can be displayed in a format appropriate for a particular currency.

AutoNumber

Can contain a value that gets automatically incremented with every new record added to a Table. It is used in fields where every value is unique and is therefore ideal for use as a Primary Key.

Yes/No

Can contain a checked box for Yes and an unchecked box for No – useful to allow the user to choose between two possible values, such as true or false; on or off; up or down; etc.

OLE Object

Can contain binary objects, such as Word documents or images, which are recreated as copies of the original files.

Hyperlink

Can contain the URL of a web page or an email address. Clicking on the URL launches a web browser that retrieves that web page or launches your default email client program.

Attachment

Can contain binary objects such as Word documents or images, which are incorporated as links to the original.

Calculated

Can contain the result of an expression that calculates a value from values contained in other fields.

With the Currency data type you can choose **Currency format** to display a currency symbol based upon Windows' Regional Settings or **Euro format** to display the € symbol irrespective of Regional Settings – neither format performs an exchange-rate conversion.

The **OLE Object** data type is quite inefficient as it creates a bitmap image of a file that is often larger than the original file. It is more efficient to use the **Attachment** data type.

Keep fields as small as possible by choosing correct data types for maximum efficiency.

Attaching objects

The Attachment data type is used to store large binary objects such as images or other Microsoft Office documents. You can attach one file or multiple files to any single record:

1 Open **Design View**, then create a new Table field of the **Attachment** data type

2 Switch to **Datasheet View**

3 Double-click the paperclip icon in the field – to open an "Attachments" dialog

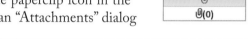

4 Click the **Add** button – to open a "Choose File" dialog

5 Navigate to the file you want to attach, then click the **Open** button on the "Choose File" dialog – to add that file to the list in the "Attachments" dialog

6 Click the **OK** button – to attach the file to the Table field

The number in brackets next to the paperclip represents the number of attached files.

To see an attachment, open the "Attachments" dialog using the above steps. Select the file you want to open, then click the **Open** button on the "Attachments" dialog. The dialog will open the file in its parent program. In the case of the above example, the **Weekly Regional Sales.xlsx** file would open in Excel.

Calculating fields

The Calculated data type automatically fills the field with the result of a formula that uses values from other fields in the Table. For example, a Table of products might contain a unit price field for each product and a quantity field for each product. A formula could multiply these two fields to automatically fill a Calculated field with a total price for each product:

1 Open **Design View**, then create fields of **AutoNumber**, **Currency**, and **Number** data types

2 Add a field of the **Calculated** data type, and you will see an "Expression Builder" dialog appear

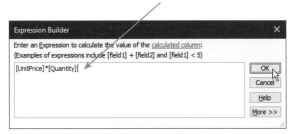

3 Now, enter a formula to multiply the fields of the **Currency** and **Number** data types using their field name

4 Click the **OK** button to close the "Expression Builder" dialog and apply the formula to the **Calculated** field

5 Switch to **Datasheet View**

6 Enter values into the fields of the **Currency** and **Number** data types – to see the Calculated field automatically filled

Expression Builder is a great feature of modern Access, which simplifies the creation formulas.

The formula appears on the **Expression** property of the General tab at the bottom of the Design View screen. Select the Expression property, then click its "..." ellipsis button to reopen the Expression Builder dialog to edit the formula.

Specifying field properties

In the Access app, every field has a set of properties that support the design of the database by enforcing rules or controlling the way in which data is presented to the user on screen. The exact number and type of properties available depends on the data type of the field in question, but most field properties are the same for all data types:

Changing field properties

1 Switch a Table to **Design View**

2 Click any field to see its "Field Properties" list appear at the bottom of the Design View screen

Hot tip

The value assigned to the **Caption** property will be displayed as a label on a Form.

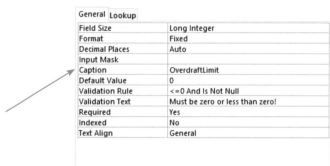

General	Lookup	
Field Size	Long Integer
Format	Fixed
Decimal Places	Auto
Input Mask	
Caption	OverdraftLimit
Default Value	0
Validation Rule	<=0 And Is Not Null
Validation Text	Must be zero or less than zero!
Required	Yes
Indexed	No
Text Align	General

3 Some properties have an ellipsis "..." button. Clicking this button usually launches a wizard or drop-down menu

Don't forget

You can click on any property to edit its value or change its settings.

General	Lookup	
Format		
Decimal Places	General Number	3456.789
Input Mask	Currency	$3,456.79
Caption	Euro	€3,456.79
Default Value	Fixed	3456.79
Validation Rule	Standard	3,456.79
Validation Text	Percent	123.00%
Required	Scientific	3.46E+03
Indexed	No	
Text Align	General	

The next few pages describe some of the more important field properties in detail and demonstrate how they can be used to ensure that only appropriate data is entered by users, or to present data to users in the correct format.

Stating Validation Rules

Validation Rules allow you to capture data in the exact ranges that you require. In optimizing database design it is important to consider business rules that govern a database (see page 36). For example, a business rule for a bank's database might be "Overdraft limits must be $0.00 or less". It is common sense to have an overdraft limit that's less than zero, but unless you explicitly state this to Access it will be unaware. In order to ensure users input only appropriate values, you can validate the data that they enter:

1 Switch a Table to **Design View**

2 Click the field to be tested for appropriate user input

3 Select the **Validation Rule** property in the "Field Properties" list, then click its "**...**" ellipsis button – to open the "Expression Builder" dialog

Caption	OverdraftLimit	
Default Value	0	
Validation Rule		...
Validation Text		

An expression that limits the values that can be entered in the field. Press F1 for help on validation rules.

4 Enter a rule into the "Expression Builder" dialog, then click its **OK** button to apply that rule

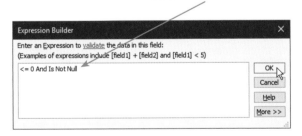

Expression Builder

Enter an Expression to validate the data in this field:
(Examples of expressions include [field1] + [field2] and [field1] < 5)

`<= 0 And Is Not Null`

OK
Cancel
Help
More >>

5 Next, select the **Validation Text** property in the "Field Properties" list, then type a message

Caption	OverdraftLimit
Default Value	0
Validation Rule	<=0 And Is Not Null
Validation Text	Must be zero or less than zero!

The error message that appears when you enter a value prohibited by the validation rule. Press F1 for help on validation text.

Hot tip

If there is already data in a Table when you enter a Validation Rule, select the **Design** tab then click the **Test Validation Rules** icon in the "Tools" group to see if the existing data complies with the new rule.

53

Don't forget

The **Validation Text** is displayed in a dialog when users try to break the Validation Rule.

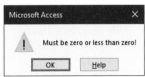

Microsoft Access

Must be zero or less than zero!

OK   Help

Creating an Input Mask

Input Masks are primarily used as a means of validating data, as they force a user to enter data in exactly the format you require. For instance, if you want the user to enter a date in **dd/mm/yyyy** format then that is what they must enter.

The Input Mask property is found on the "Field Properties" list at the bottom of the Design View screen:

The **Input Mask** Wizard only works with Text and Date data types, not Number or Currency.

1 Click the field to which you want to assign an **Input Mask**

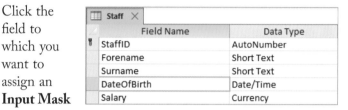

Field Name	Data Type
StaffID	AutoNumber
Forename	Short Text
Surname	Short Text
DateOfBirth	Date/Time
Salary	Currency

2 Type the required **Input Mask** into the property list

The "0" character in the Input Mask tells Access to accept only a single digit at that point. The "/" character is a special character for separating dates. You can use Access **Help** to find out more about the Input Mask characters.

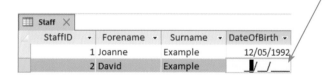

General	Lookup
Format	Short Date
Input Mask	00/00/0000
Caption	

Click here to launch the Input Mask Wizard

3 Users must now enter data in the "DateOfBirth" field in the format demanded by the **Input Mask**, as shown here

StaffID	Forename	Surname	DateOfBirth
1	Joanne	Example	12/05/1992
2	David	Example	/_/___

After the data is entered in the required format, Access will display it in the Format property specified for that field (for example, the "Short Date" format shown in the first record above). If the user doesn't enter data in the required format, a dialog will politely point out the error:

Assign "Password" to the **Input Mask** property to hide the data being entered. No matter what the user types in, only asterisks (*) will be displayed on screen.

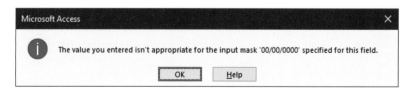

Microsoft Access

The value you entered isn't appropriate for the input mask '00/00/0000' specified for this field.

OK   Help

Defining a Default Value

Sometimes it is useful to define a Default Value for a field. There might perhaps be a certain value that needs to be entered more often than not – such as "Female" rather than "Male". For example, a marketing survey undertaken by a bookstore might show that women are more likely to buy books from their store than men. Therefore, it would make processing new customer details quicker if "Female" were the default value for the "Sex" field of the bookstore's "Customer" Table:

1 Switch to **Design View**

2 Select the field to be assigned a default value

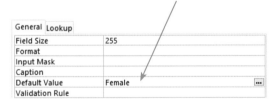

Customer ✕	
Field Name	**Data Type**
🔑 CustomerID	AutoNumber
Forename	Short Text
Surname	Short Text
Sex	Short Text

3 Type the required **Default Value** into the property list

General Lookup		
Field Size	255	
Format		
Input Mask		
Caption		
Default Value	Female	⋯
Validation Rule		

4 Switch to **Datasheet View**, and see the default value you entered appear every time you start a new record

Customer ✕			
CustomerID ▾	Forename ▾	Surname ▾	Sex ▾
1	Susan	McKenzie	Female
* (New)			Female

The **Default Value** and many other field properties can also be changed in Datasheet View – select the **Fields** tab, then explore the "Properties" and "Field Validation" groups.

55

After changing field properties, click the **Save** button on the Quick Access Toolbar to keep your changes.

Referencing Indexes

An Access "Index" is simply a reference that points to the physical location where a piece of data is stored. An Index greatly improves the speed with which Access finds and sorts data within a Table. The principle is similar to that of an index in a book. For example, you might want to find every place the term "Save icon" is mentioned in this book. Rather than laboriously searching every page looking for that term, it is more sensible to go to the back of the book and find the relevant pages from the book's index:

Any **Primary Key** field will be automatically indexed by Access, but it is good practice to index **Foreign Key** fields too. You can index any field if it is unique or if its values are likely to be different from each other.

1 Open the Table that you want to create Indexes for in **Design View**

2 Click the **Design** tab on the Ribbon

3 Click the **Indexes** icon in the "Show/Hide" group – to open an "Indexes" dialog

4 Click the **Index Name** field in an empty row

5 Type the name of the Index

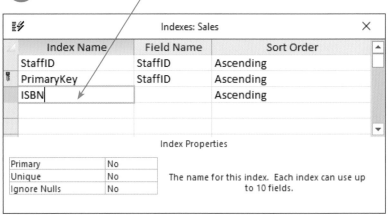

Indexes: Sales			
Index Name	Field Name	Sort Order	
StaffID	StaffID	Ascending	
PrimaryKey	StaffID	Ascending	
ISBN		Ascending	

Index Properties

Primary	No	
Unique	No	The name for this index. Each index can use up to 10 fields.
Ignore Nulls	No	

Creating too many **Indexes** in a Table can slow down some tasks.

6 Press the Tab key to move to the next field

7 Choose a field to index from the drop-down menu

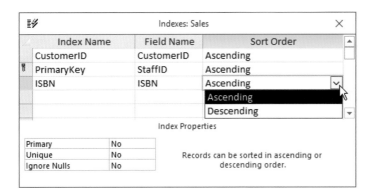

8 Choose the sort order you prefer

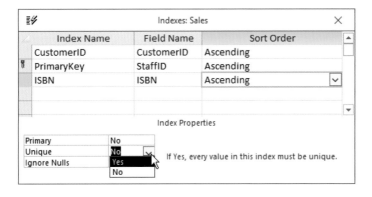

Hot tip

To delete an Index, right-click the Index you want to delete, then choose the **Delete Rows** option from the context menu that appears.

9 Identify the field as unique, if appropriate

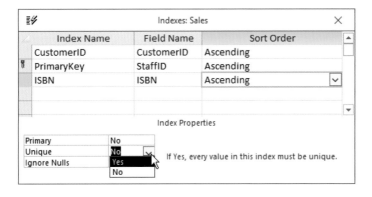

Providing a Lookup Column

With a "Lookup Column" users enter predetermined values into a cell by selecting options from a drop-down menu, rather than typing in a value themselves. This helps minimize errors caused by incorrectly-spelled words.

The values in a Lookup Column can either be drawn from another Table (hence the term "lookup") or given to Access when the Lookup Column is created. The example below follows the latter option:

1 Switch to **Design View**, then select an empty field that you want to become a **Lookup Column**

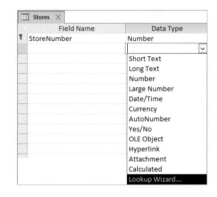

2 Click the arrow button in the **Data Type** column and choose the **Lookup Wizard...** option

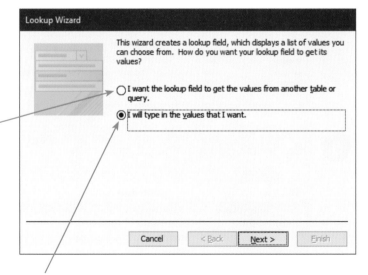

3 Check the second option to type in values manually

4 Click the **Next** button to continue

5 Specify the number of columns you want to include in the Lookup Column

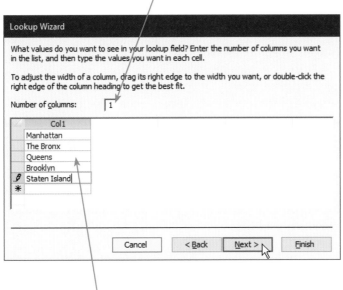

Having more than one column displayed in a **Lookup Column** can make the user options more descriptive. For example, a Lookup Column for addresses could display a column for each element of an address.

6 Type a list of values from which users will be able to select, then click the **Next** button to continue

7 Type a name for your Lookup Column, then click the **Finish** button to create the Lookup Column

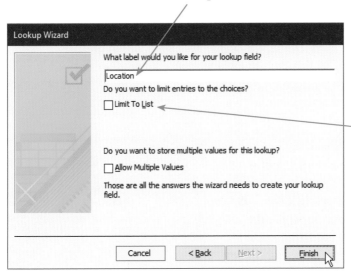

Be sure to check the **Limit To List** option if you want to completely prohibit users from typing other text entries.

...cont'd

Click a cell in the Lookup Column, then choose a value from the drop-down menu to enter it:

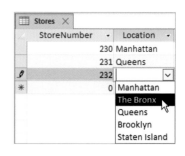

Using multiple values

A great feature of Access is the ability to store multiple values in one field. This is useful if you have a range of options from which to select a value but more than one is appropriate. For example, suppose each bookstore branch specializes in particular genres of books. Being able to enter each genre that's applicable to a branch into a multiple value Lookup Column would be an ideal solution. To create a multiple value Lookup Column follow the steps for creating a Lookup Column on pages 58-59, but additionally check the option to "Allow Multiple Values" in Step 7, shown on page 59:

Storing multiple values in a single field might seem to be against the principles of good database design, but **Access** doesn't physically store the values in one field – it hides them away in system Tables as separate fields.

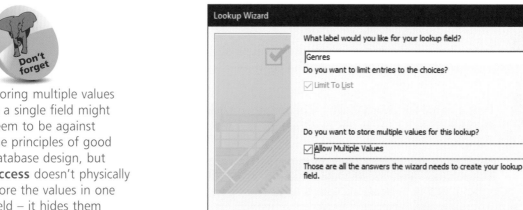

Check the box of each value you want to store in the field, then click the **OK** button. Here, the Manhattan store specializes in Horror and Sci-Fi:

4

Defining Relationships

The Relationships window

The Relationships window in Access allows you to lay out your Tables and specify relationships between them visually:

The Relationships window is improved so you can easily grab and resize the table borders.

Tables are depicted in boxes

Primary Key fields are denoted by key icons

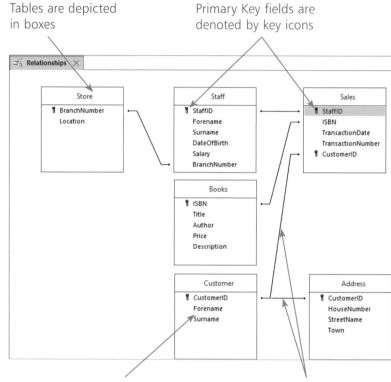

You can save the layout of the Relationships window at any time by clicking the **Save** icon on the Quick Access Toolbar, or by right-clicking the Relationships window and choosing the **Save Layout** option on the context menu.

Fields are listed within the Table boxes

Relationships are represented by connecting lines

Opening the Relationships window

You can remove everything from the Relationships window by clicking the **Clear Layout** icon in the "Tools" group on the Ribbon's **Design** tab.

① Open the Tables for which you want you want to create relationships – in the **Tables** window

② Select the **Database Tools** tab on the Ribbon

③ Click the **Relationships** icon in the "Relationships" group

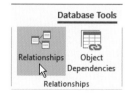

...cont'd

Adding Tables
If no Tables have been assigned to the Relationships window,
Access prompts you to add some with the "Show Table" dialog:

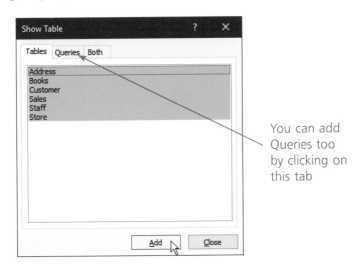

You can add
Queries too
by clicking on
this tab

The "Show Table" dialog
can be summoned at
any point by clicking the
Show Table icon in
the "Relationships"
group on the
Ribbon's
Design tab.

Show
Table

1 Select the **Tables** you want to add

2 Click the **Add** button – to add your selection

3 Click the **Close** button – to close the dialog

Tables are arranged by clicking and holding the left mouse button
on their headings, then dragging them to where they're needed:

You can remove a Table
from the Relationships
window at any time
by clicking the **Hide
Table** icon in the
"Relationships" group on
the Ribbon's
Design tab.

Hide Table

The goal, once the relationships have been specified, is to have a
screen that is uncluttered and can be easily read.

Specifying relationships

Relationships are specified between Tables by clicking and dragging a field (usually the Primary Key) to a corresponding field in another Table. The two fields that you want to relate must share the same data type, or Access will display an error message:

1 Click and hold the field name of a **Primary Key**

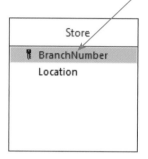
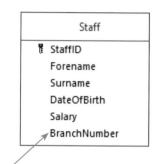

2 Drag it across to the **Foreign Key** of the second Table

3 Release the mouse button to see Access display the "Edit Relationships" dialog

Notice that **Access** tells you the type of relationship you are specifying.

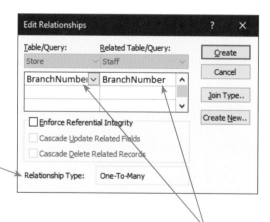

4 Ensure that the correct fields are to be related

5 If necessary, the fields can be changed by clicking here and selecting different fields from the drop-down menu

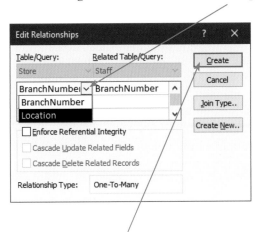

6 Click the **Create** button to make the relationship

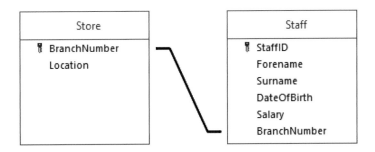

A relationship between Tables is denoted in Access by a black line linking two fields, as shown in the illustration above.

Although the "Edit Relationships" dialog describes the type of relationship created between the two Tables, it's still important to recognize the difference between the different relationship types in order for you to make the correct connections between Tables – One-to-One, One-to-Many, or Many-to-Many (see pages 30-31).

Hot tip

You can open the "Edit Relationships" dialog by right-clicking on a relationship line and selecting **Edit Relationships** from the context menu.

Enforcing integrity

When a record in a Table is no longer needed it seems rational to delete it and, in some situations, it might seem like a good idea to change the value or data type of a Primary Key. These actions can, however, cause update and deletion anomalies that interfere with the performance of the database, and may cause errors.

To safeguard against this, you can enforce referential integrity. This ensures that a record in one Table only ever refers to an existing record in another Table. To enforce referential integrity, you must first open the "Edit Relationships" dialog (see page 64):

1 Select the connecting line between the related fields, by clicking on the line with the left mouse button

2 Click the **Edit Relationships** icon in the "Tools" group on the Ribbon's **Design** tab

3 Check the **Enforce Referential Integrity** option

Clicking the **Relationship Report** icon generates a printable version of the Relationships window.

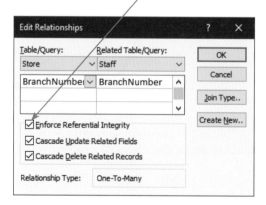

4 Next, check the **Cascade Update Related Fields** option

5 Now, check the **Cascade Delete Related Records** option

6 Click the **OK** button to apply the edits to the relationship

The connecting line between the related fields will now have a "1" symbol next to the parent Table and an "infinity" symbol next to the child Table, as shown in the illustration below:

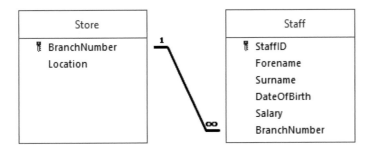

These edits produce certain actions within the database:

Enforce Referential Integrity

Referential integrity is a "constraint" imposed on a Table to maintain the accuracy and consistency of data in your database. By enforcing referential integrity, you are asking Access to make sure that a record in one Table that refers to a related record in another Table only ever refers to an existing record.

Another type of constraint is the entity integrity constraint, which states that no Primary Key value can be null. When you make a field the Primary Key, Access makes sure that a user inputs a value into it.

Cascade Update Related Fields

This option forces Access to update all related child records when you change the value in a Primary Key field.

Cascade Delete Related Records

This option forces Access to delete all related child records when you delete a record.

It is typically a good idea to select the options to **Enforce Referential Integrity**, **Cascade Update Related Fields**, and **Cascade Delete Related Records**.

Specifying Join properties

As well as specifying relationships between Tables, you can also specify "Join" types. The Join type is used by Queries to decide which records should be displayed when the Query is run. It can easily be selected from within the "Edit Relationships" dialog:

1 Click on the connecting line relating two Tables

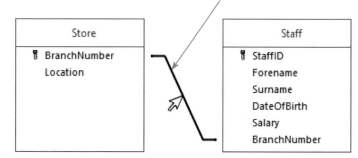

Beware

You must click precisely on the connecting line to make the selection!

2 Click the **Edit Relationships** icon in the "Tools" group on the Ribbon's **Design** tab – to open the "Edit Relationships" dialog

3 Next, click the **Join Type...** button on the "Edit Relationships" dialog – to open the "Join Properties" dialog

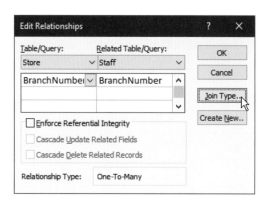

4 Now, select the type of **Join** you want to use from the "Join Properties" dialog options

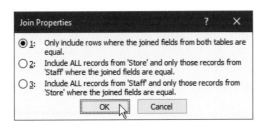

5 Click the **OK** button to apply your selection and to close the "Join Properties" dialog

More about Join types

The "Join Properties" dialog lets you specify two different types of join – the Inner Join (option 1 of the dialog) and the Outer Join (options 2 and 3 of the dialog):

- **Inner Join** – ensures that only those records where there is an exact match between the related fields will be displayed.

- **Outer Join** – ensures that a Query will display all the records from one Table, but only those records from another Table where the related fields match. For example, running a Query based on the Tables below would display all records from the "Customer" Table but only those from the "Sales" Table where both "CustomerID" fields match.

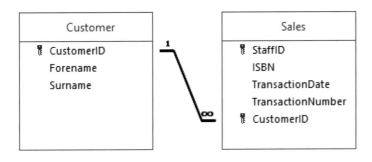

The default type of Join is an **Inner Join**, which displays only records where there is an exact match between the related fields.

Directing Joins

When you specify an Outer Join between Tables, Access modifies the relationship line to include an arrow – the direction of which is dependent on the type of Outer Join you have selected.

Left Join

An arrow pointing to the "Many" side of a relationship indicates a Left Join. A Query based on a Left Join will display all the records on the "One" side of the relationship, and only those records from the "Many" side where there is an exact match. An example of a Query based on a Left Join is shown below:

The procedure for making Queries is described later (in Chapter 6) but it is important to understand here that **Join** types in relationships do affect which data is returned in the Query result.

CustomerID ▾	Forename ▾	Surname ▾	TransactionDate ▾
1	Mike	McGrath	Dec-01-22
2	Anne	Smith	Dec-01-22
3	Tony	Jones	
4	Leslie	Phillips	
5	John	Dee	Dec-02-22
6	Shirley	Peel	
7	Ellie	Howard	Dec-05-22

Customer Query - Left Join

Data in the "CustomerID", "Forename", and "Surname" fields is taken from the "Customer" Table on page 69. Data in the "TransactionDate" field is taken from the related "Sales" Table on page 69. Notice that not all the records contain data for the "TransactionDate" field.

Right Join

An arrow pointing to the "One" side of a relationship indicates a Right Join. A Query based on a Right Join will display the opposite to that of a Left Join. The example above will then see a fully-populated "TransactionDate" field, but only some of the fields from the "Customer" Table will contain data:

Customer Query - Right Join

CustomerID ▾	Forename ▾	Surname ▾	TransactionDate ▾
1	Mike	McGrath	Dec-01-22
2	Anne	Smith	Dec-01-22
5	John	Dee	Dec-02-22
7	Ellie	Howard	Dec-05-22

5 Handling Data

This chapter demonstrates how to insert data by direct entry or import from external sources; how to export data; and how to filter data.

Entering data

There are many different ways to populate your Access database with data. The most obvious way of inputting data is by direct entry into a Table – simply typing a value into a cell. You can also copy and paste data from other programs, such as Microsoft Excel, or import existing data from another database:

Direct entry

ID	Forename	Surname	Position
1	Betty	Slocombe	Senior Sales Assistant
2	Shirley	Brahms	Junior Sales Assistant
3	Ernest	Grainger	Senior Sales Assistant
4	Wilberforce	Humphries	Junior Sales Assistant
5	James	Lucas	Junior Sales Assistant
6	Stephen	Peacock	Floor Manager
(New)			

Staff

1 Select the cell where you want to enter a value, by clicking it with the left mouse button

ID	Forename	Surname	Position
1	Betty	Slocombe	Senior Sales Assistant
2	Shirley	Brahms	Junior Sales Assistant
3	Ernest	Grainger	Senior Sales Assistant
4	Wilberforce	Humphries	Junior Sales Assistant
5	James	Lucas	Junior Sales Assistant
6	Stephen	Peacock	Floor Manager
7	Diana		
(New)			

Staff

2 Type the value into the selected cell

3 Press the **Tab** key to confirm your entry

4 See the next cell to the right become automatically selected, ready for you to type another entry in that record

5 Select a cell in another record where you want to enter a value, then repeat the previous steps

Hot tip

You can use the **Tab** key to move along the cells of a record, and also use the arrow keys to move around Table cells.

Hot tip

Access has an **AutoCorrect** feature that can change the text you enter and is enabled by default. If you prefer to disable AutoCorrect, click **File**, **Options**, **Proofing**, **AutoCorrect Options**, then uncheck all the checkboxes.

72

Inserting records

When you've finished entering data into the very last Table row, Access will automatically insert a new empty row for you. However, you can manually insert a new Table row at any time:

1 Click the **New** icon in the "Records" group on the Ribbon's **Home** tab

Refresh All ▾	New	Σ Totals
	Save	ABC Spelling
	✕ Delete ▾	More ▾
	Records	

Resizing Table rows

You can easily resize the rows of a Table for clarity:

1 Put the cursor between two rows in the **Row Selector**

Staff ✕			
ID ▾	Forename ▾	Surname ▾	Position ▾
1	Betty	Slocombe	Senior Sales Assistant
2	Shirley	Brahms	Junior Sales Assistant
3	Ernest	Grainger	Senior Sales Assistant
4	Wilberforce	Humphries	Junior Sales Assistant
5	James	Lucas	Junior Sales Assistant

2 Click and hold the left mouse button – see a black line appear between the two rows

3 Drag the mouse up to decrease the size of all rows, or drag down to increase the size of all rows

Staff ✕			
ID ▾	Forename ▾	Surname ▾	Position ▾
1	Betty	Slocombe	Senior Sales Assistant
2	Shirley	Brahms	Junior Sales Assistant
3	Ernest	Grainger	Senior Sales Assistant
4	Wilberforce	Humphries	Junior Sales Assistant
5	James	Lucas	Junior Sales Assistant

Beware

You can only resize the rows by using the **Row Selector** column, not by using field columns.

Using the Clipboard

The "Clipboard" group on the Ribbon's Home tab provides all the functions you need to copy and paste data:

The Microsoft Office Clipboard

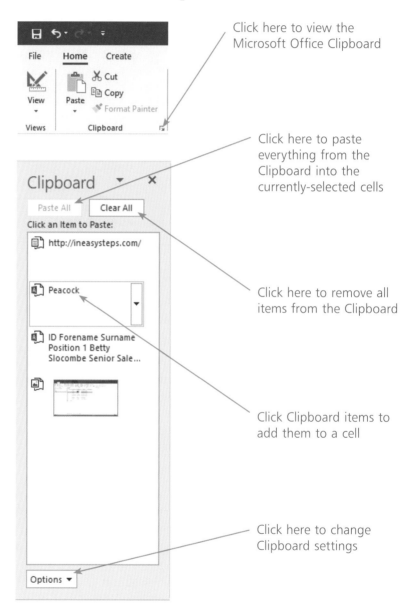

Click here to view the Microsoft Office Clipboard

Click here to paste everything from the Clipboard into the currently-selected cells

Click here to remove all items from the Clipboard

Click Clipboard items to add them to a cell

Click here to change Clipboard settings

Don't forget

The **Clipboard** lists all items you copy onto the Clipboard from any app – you are not limited to only Access items. For example, a URL copied from your web browser's address field will appear on the Clipboard.

The Clipboard icon group explained

Clicking here pastes data onto the selected cell

Clicking here copies and then deletes the data

Clicking here copies style formatting, not the data itself

Clicking here copies data but does not delete the data

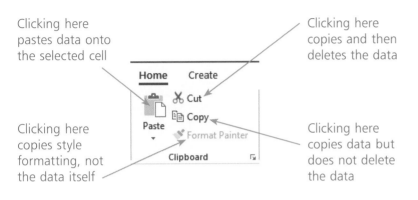

Beware

Icons in the "Clipboard" group will appear grayed-out unless their functionality is available. **Format Painter** is unavailable in these screenshots as its Access functionality is only available when a selected item contains style formatting – raw data contains only data type formatting.

Copying data between cells

ID	Forename	Surname	Position	Salary
1	Betty	Slocombe	Senior Sales Assistant	$25,000.00
2	Shirley	Brahms	Junior Sales Assistant	$20,000.00
3	Ernest	Grainger	Senior Sales Assistant	$25,000.00
4	Wilberforce	Humphries	Junior Sales Assistant	$20,000.00
5	James	Lucas	Junior Sales Assistant	$20,000.00
6	Stephen	Peacock	Floor Manager	$35,000.00
7	Diana	Yardswick	Canteen Manager	$15,000.00
8	Peter	Broom	Maintenance Manager	

1 Select the data you wish to copy

2 Click the **Copy** icon in the "Clipboard" group – to copy the selected data to the Clipboard

3 Select the cell in which you want to paste the data

4 Click the **Paste** icon – to paste the copied data from the Clipboard into the selected cell

Hot tip

Alternatively, you can use the **Copy** and **Paste** options on the right-click context menu to copy selected data from one cell to another cell.

	6	Stephen	Peacock	Floor Manager	$35,000.00
	7	Diana	Yardswick	Canteen Manager	$15,000.00
	8	Peter	Broom	Maintenance Manager	$15,000.00
*	(New)				$0.00

75

Copying data to/from Excel

It is often desirable to use Access data within Excel. For instance, you might want to see data from a sales Table in an Excel spreadsheet to examine performance in a particular quarter. Previously, using Access data within Excel involved a time-consuming export task, but with modern Access it can be achieved in a couple of clicks:

1 In Access, click one or more **Table** field heading to select the data you want to copy to Excel

⊞ Staff ✕				
ID ▾	Forename ▾	Surname ▾	Position ▾	Salary ▾
1	Betty	Slocombe	Senior Sales Assistant	$25,000.00
2	Shirley	Brahms	Junior Sales Assistant	$20,000.00
3	Ernest	Grainger	Senior Sales Assistant	$25,000.00
4	Wilberforce	Humphries	Junior Sales Assistant	$20,000.00
5	James	Lucas	Junior Sales Assistant	$20,000.00
6	Stephen	Peacock	Floor Manager	$35,000.00
7	Diana	Yardswick	Canteen Manager	$15,000.00
8	Peter	Broom	Maintenance Manager	$15,000.00
*	(New)			$0.00

Beware

Data copied into Excel may be formatted according to the default formatting currently selected in Excel. This means that your data from Access might look different when viewed in Excel. Consult the Microsoft Excel **Help** documentation if you want to change the default formatting.

2 Click the **Copy** icon in the Ribbon's "Clipboard" group

3 Click the Excel cell in which the first field will be copied

A1	▾	⋮
	A	B
1		
2		

4 In Excel, click the **Paste** icon (it's the same as the Paste icon in Access) to insert the copied rows into Excel

	A	B	C	D
1	Forename	Surname	Position	Salary
2	Betty	Slocombe	Senior Sales Assistant	$25,000.00
3	Shirley	Brahms	Junior Sales Assistant	$20,000.00
4	Ernest	Grainger	Senior Sales Assistant	$25,000.00
5	Wilberforce	Humphries	Junior Sales Assistant	$20,000.00
6	James	Lucas	Junior Sales Assistant	$20,000.00
7	Stephen	Peacock	Floor Manager	$35,000.00
8	Diana	Yardswick	Canteen Manageress	$15,000.00
9	Peter	Broom	Maintenance Manager	$15,000.00
10				

It is now possible to copy data into your Tables directly from Microsoft Excel in a few easy steps. You can copy single cell data, or multiple rows and columns of data, from Excel into Access:

1 In Excel, select the cells you want to copy

9	8	Peter	Broom	Maintenance Manager	$15,000.00
10	9	Alice	Watson	Trainee Sales Assistant	$10,000.00
11	10	Zoe	Tibbs	Trainee Sales Assistant	$10,000.00

2 In Excel, click the **Copy** icon (it's the same as the Copy icon in Access)

3 In Access, highlight the fields or rows that the data will be pasted into by clicking field headings or by using the **Row Selector**

	7	Diana	Yardswick	Canteen Manageress	$15,000.00
	8	Peter	Broom	Maintenance Manager	$15,000.00
*	0				$0.00

4 Click the **Paste** icon in the Access Ribbon's "Clipboard" group – to see a warning dialog appear

> **Microsoft Access**   ✕
>
> ⚠ You are about to paste 2 record(s).
>
> Are you sure you want to paste these records?
>
> [Yes]   [No]

5 Click the **Yes** button on the dialog to paste the data

	7	Diana	Yardswick	Canteen Manageress	$15,000.00
	8	Peter	Broom	Maintenance Manager	$15,000.00
	9	Alice	Watson	Trainee Sales Assistant	$10,000.00
	10	Zoe	Tibbs	Trainee Sales Assistant	$10,000.00
*	0				$0.00

Hot tip

You can copy as much or as little data as you desire from Excel.

77

Don't forget

The Excel cell data will need to match the permitted Access field data to avoid a "Paste Error". For example, a numeric column has been added to the Excel worksheet here because the first Access field here must contain a Number.

Importing data from Excel

You might sometimes want to import data from an Excel file. Perhaps your database is used to track your customers, whose details are recorded in an Excel spreadsheet. Rather than type the customer details into Access using a printed Excel spreadsheet, you could simply append the details to a Table or use the spreadsheet data to create a completely new Table in Access.

When importing from Excel it's important that the spreadsheet you are importing data from is in the correct format. Set up the spreadsheet so that each row in Excel is equivalent to a row in Access and each column is equivalent to a field, as shown below:

Don't forget

Imported data gets translated from the foreign-source format into an Access database data type format.

	A	B	C	D	E	F	G	H
1	CustomerID	Forename	Surname					
2	1	Adrian	Young					
3	2	Boris	Klein					
4	3	Colin	Farrow					
5	4	Dennis	Lewis					
6	5	Edward	Monk					

Importing data into a new Table

1 In Access, click the **External Data** tab on the Ribbon

2 Next, click the **New Data Source** icon in the Ribbon's "Import & Link" group

3 Select the **From File**, **Excel** option

4 When the "Get External Data" dialog appears, be sure to select the **Import the source data into a new table in the current database** option

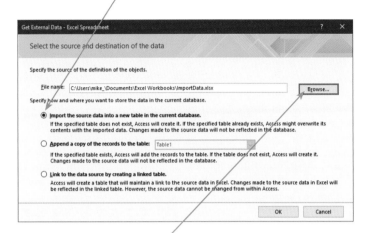

Hot tip

Notice that the second option on the "Get External Data" dialog allows you to append imported data to an existing Access Table.

5 Click the **Browse...** button to display the "File Open" dialog

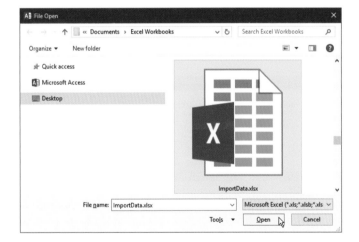

6 Select the Excel file to import data from, then click the **Open** button – to close the "File Open" dialog

7 Click the **OK** button on the "Get External Data" dialog – to open the "Import Spreadsheet Wizard"

...cont'd

8 Select the worksheet to be imported by clicking on it

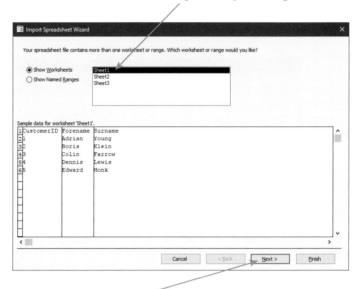

9 Click the **Next** button to continue

10 If you want the values in the first row to be used as field names in your new Table, be sure to check this option

Don't forget

If importing data to append to an existing **Table** that already has field headings, you do not need to use the column headings in the spreadsheet's first row.

11 Click the **Next** button to continue

12 Click here to change field names

13 Click here to change data types

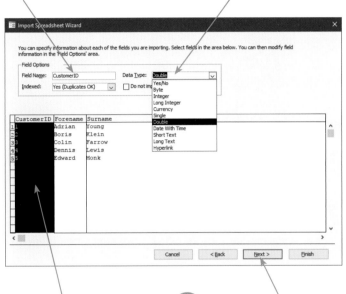

Beware

Think carefully about the selections you make on this page. It's quicker and easier to choose the right data types now rather than later.

14 Click a column to select that field

15 Click the **Next** button to continue

16 Let Access add a Primary Key, or use the drop-down menu to choose one, then click the **Next** button

Hot tip

When you click a column to select it, the background for that column will turn black to denote it is selected.

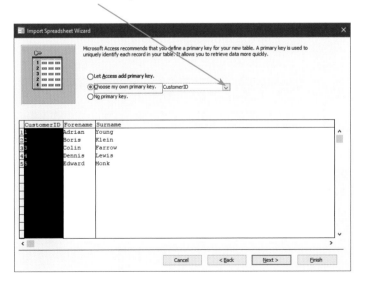

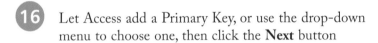

...cont'd

Hot tip

After importing data into a Table, you can use the **Analyze Table** tool in the "Analyze" group on the **Database Tools** tab to have Access suggest how to split the Table to create relationships – but the suggestion may not be the best solution.

 Type a name for your new Table

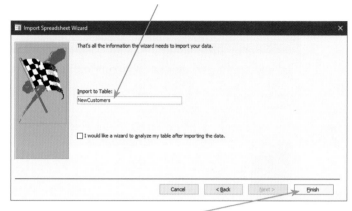

 Click the **Finish** button – to exit the "Import Spreadsheet Wizard" and see the "Get External Data" dialog reappear

 In order to easily import from the same worksheet in the future, be sure to check the **Save import steps** option

Hot tip

The procedure to implement the **Saved Import** steps, to actually import data from an external source, is described on page 87.

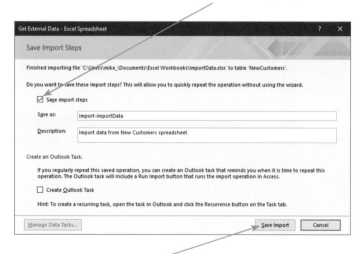

 Click the **Save Import** button – to save your import steps in a list of "Saved Imports" associated with the Table

Importing data from Access

There are two ways of working with other Access databases. The first is to import database objects, such as Tables, Queries, and Forms, from a database. The second is to link to a Table in another Access database. The first method gives you a great degree of control over what you import. For example, you can import either a Table and its data, or just the structure of the Table:

Importing database objects

1 In Access, click the **External Data** tab on the Ribbon

2 Next, click the **New Data Source** icon in the Ribbon's "Import & Link" group

3 Select the **From Database, Access** menu options

4 When the "Get External Data" dialog appears, be sure to select the **Import tables, queries, forms, reports, macros, and modules into the current database** option

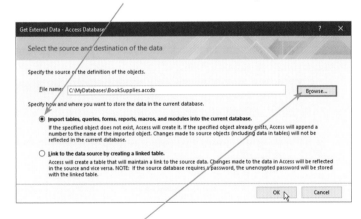

5 Use the **Browse...** button to select the database you wish to import objects from

6 Click the **OK** button to continue, and see the "Import Objects" dialog appear

Hot tip

The procedure to import database objects from an Access database is similar to that for importing data from an Excel spreadsheet.

NEW

The ability to import from dBASE files was reintroduced in the modern Access app.

Don't forget

The **Browse...** button launches the "File Open" dialog so you can navigate to an Access database file for selection.

...cont'd

Hot tip

You can select more than one Table in the "Import Objects" dialog.

7 Click the tabs to see the available objects

8 Select the names of the objects to import

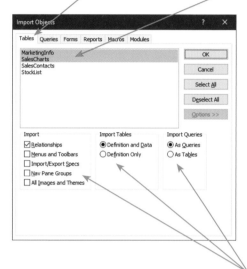

9 Click the **Options** button, then choose import options

10 Click the **OK** button to continue

11 In order to easily import from the same database in the future, be sure to check the **Save import steps** option

Hot tip

The procedure to implement the **Saved Import** steps, to actually import data from an external source, is described on page 87.

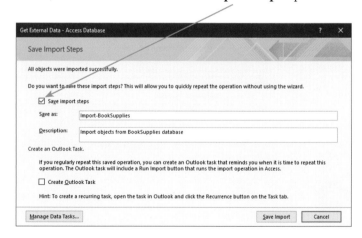

12 Click the **Save Import** button – to save your import steps in a list of "Saved Imports" associated with the Table

Linking to an Access database

Repeatedly importing data from one database into another is inefficient and wasteful. If there is data in another database that you need to use regularly, it might be best to link it with a Table in your own database. By linking two Tables, a connection is made between the original Table (the source) and a Table in your own database (the destination):

It is only possible to link Tables; not Forms, Queries, or any other database object.

1. In Access, click the **External Data** tab on the Ribbon

2. Next, click the **New Data Source** icon in the Ribbon's "Import & Link" group

3. Select the **From Database, Access** option

4. When the "Get External Data" dialog appears, select the **Link to the data source by creating a linked table** option

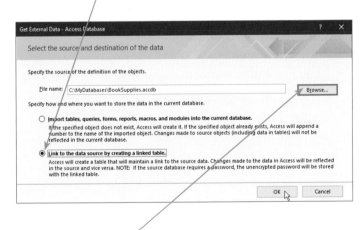

5. Use the **Browse...** button to select the database containing Tables you wish to link

6. Click the **OK** button to continue, and see the "Link Tables" dialog appear

Once a Table is linked to a counterpart in another database, you can view and change the values in it as you like. The changes you make will be seen in both Tables. The only thing you can't do is change the structure of the Table.

...cont'd

7 Select the names of the Tables you want to link to in the source database

Hot tip

You can select more than one Table in the "Link Tables" dialog.

8 Click the **OK** button to create the links

Don't forget

You can update linked Tables at any time by using the **Linked Table Manager**. This icon is located in the "Import & Link" group on the Ribbon's **External Data** tab, and the process is described on page 185.

The names of the linked Tables now appear in the Navigation Pane, and they can be opened and used just like any other Table.

Linked Tables are distinguished from other Tables in the Navigation Pane by an arrow that appears beside the Table name.

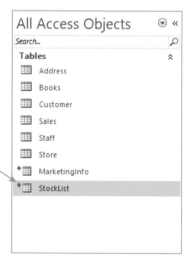

Managing import tasks

If you chose to save your import steps, you may have wondered where they are saved. You can find them using the "Manage Data Tasks" dialog:

1 Click the **Saved Imports** icon in the "Import & Link" group on the Ribbon's **External Data** tab – to open the "Manage Data Tasks" dialog

2 Click the **Saved Imports** tab, then choose an import task

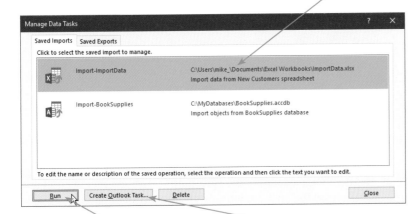

3 Click the **Run** button to implement the import steps

4 See a confirmation message on completion – click **OK** to close the message dialog

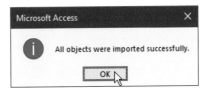

5 Refer to the **Navigation Pane** to see the imported items have now been added to the current database

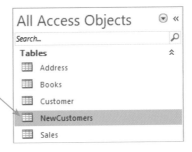

Notice that the data source of the import/export task is accompanied by a program icon to help ensure you're choosing the right data source.

You can click the **Create Outlook Task...** button if you'd like to be reminded to repeat an import/export task that is frequently required.

Exporting data from Access

All Access database objects can be exported in a variety of file formats that allow data in a Table to be used in another program, or simply presented for information purposes. Access exports to the same file formats as those it imports, plus it can export Tables to Portable Document Format (PDF) documents, XML Paper Specification (XPS) documents, and Microsoft Word documents.

Table data is most frequently exported from Access for use within an Excel spreadsheet:

Exporting Table data to Excel

1 In Access, open the **Table** you want to export data from

ISBN	Book Title
9781840788402	C Programming in easy steps
9781840787191	C# Programming in easy steps
9781840787573	C++ Programming in easy steps
9781840786422	Coding for Beginners in easy steps
9781840787375	Excel VBA in easy steps
9781840787535	Java in easy steps
9781840788273	PHP & MySQL in easy steps
9781840788129	Python in easy steps
9781840785432	SQL in easy steps
9781840787016	Visual Basic in easy steps

Books ✕

2 Next, click the **External Data** tab on the Ribbon

Icons are provided on the **External Data** tab for the most popular export formats, but further options are available from the **More** drop-down menu.

3 Now, click the **Excel** icon in the "Export" group – to open the "Export - Excel Spreadsheet" dialog

4 Select a file name and format from the drop-down menu

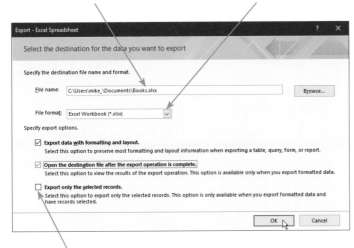

By default, the Excel file will be given the same name as the **Table** containing the data being exported.

5 Select any required options, then click the **OK** button to export the data to Excel

▲	A	B
1	**ISBN**	**Book Title**
2	9781840788402	C Programming in easy steps
3	9781840787191	C# Programming in easy steps
4	9781840787573	C++ Programming in easy steps
5	9781840786422	Coding for Beginners in easy steps
6	9781840787375	Excel VBA in easy steps
7	9781840787535	Java in easy steps
8	9781840788273	PHP & MySQL in easy steps
9	9781840788129	Python in easy steps
10	9781840785432	SQL in easy steps
11	9781840787016	Visual Basic in easy steps

Cell formatting may need to be amended after exporting to Excel in order to represent the data correctly. For example, the ISBN column may need to have a **Number** format.

6 Check the **Save export steps** option – to save your export steps in a list of "Saved Exports" associated with the Table

Export - Excel Spreadsheet

Save Export Steps

Finished exporting 'Books' to file 'C:\Users\mike_\Documents\Books.xlsx' successfully.

Do you want to save these export steps? This will allow you to quickly repeat the operation without using the wizard.

☑ Save export steps

Save as: Export-Books

Description: Export books table to Excel

...cont'd

Exporting Table data to Word

1 In Access, open the **Table** you want to export data from

ISBN	Book Title
9781840788402	C Programming in easy steps
9781840787191	C# Programming in easy steps
9781840787573	C++ Programming in easy steps
9781840786422	Coding for Beginners in easy steps
9781840787375	Excel VBA in easy steps
9781840787535	Java in easy steps
9781840788273	PHP & MySQL in easy steps
9781840788129	Python in easy steps
9781840785432	SQL in easy steps
9781840787016	Visual Basic in easy steps

Books ×

2 Next, click the **External Data** tab on the Ribbon

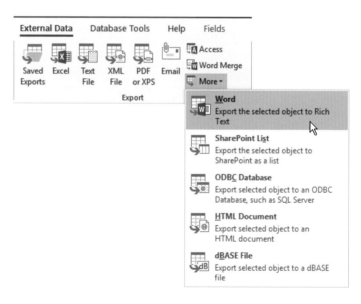

Exporting data as an **XML File** or as a **Text File** allows the data to be useful in many other apps. Exporting a Text File without preserving formatting provides an option to format the Table data as a comma-delimited file.

3 Now, click the **More** icon in the "Export" group – to open a drop-down menu of export options

4 Select the **Word** option – to open the "Export - RTF File" dialog

5 Select a file name and folder location

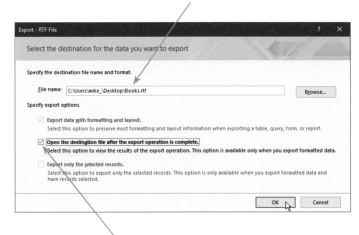

Data can only be exported as a Table in a **Rich Text Format** (**RTF**) file, not in other Word file formats.

6 Select any required options, then click the **OK** button to export the data to Word

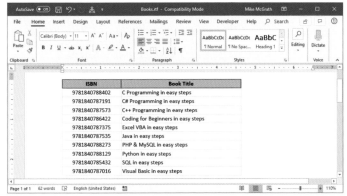

7 Check the **Save export steps** option – to save your export steps in a list of "Saved Exports" associated with the Table

You must give the **Saved Export** a unique name – to avoid overwriting other Saved Exports.

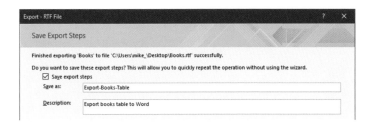

...cont'd

Access database objects can be exported for attachment to email in a variety of formats, so you can easily share data with colleagues. Usefully, the data can also be inserted into an HTML template using special tags for attachment to an email message:

Exporting Table data to email

After typing the tags, this HTML template file is saved on the desktop as **template.html** – alongside an image file named **logo.png**.

1 Open a plain text editor, such as **Notepad**, then create an HTML template using special Access template tags

```
<html> <head>
<title> <!--AccessTemplate_Title--> </title>
</head> <body>
<p> <img src="logo.png">
<br>We have some great programming titles...</p>
<!--AccessTemplate_Body-->
</body> </html>
```

2 In Access, open the Table you want to export data from

▦ Books ×	
ISBN ▾	**Book Title** ▾
9781840788402	C Programming in easy steps
9781840787191	C# Programming in easy steps
9781840787573	C++ Programming in easy steps
9781840786422	Coding for Beginners in easy steps
9781840787375	Excel VBA in easy steps
9781840787535	Java in easy steps
9781840788273	PHP & MySQL in easy steps
9781840788129	Python in easy steps
9781840785432	SQL in easy steps
9781840787016	Visual Basic in easy steps

3 Next, click the **External Data** tab on the Ribbon

4 Now, click the **Email** icon in the "Export" group – to open the "Send Object As" dialog

...cont'd

5 In the dialog, select the **HTML** output format

6 Click the **OK** button to continue

7 Check the **Select a HTML Template** option

8 Browse to the template file you created earlier

9 Click the **OK** button to create the attachment

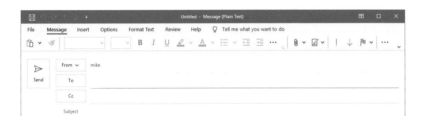

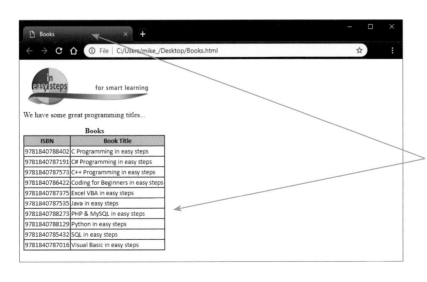

Hot tip

The HTML attachment comprises the template content and data inserted by Access to replace the special template tags.

Filtering data

You may sometimes want to limit the amount of data on screen. For example, in a Sales Table you might only want to view data about a particular product. Filters provide this ability, and can be found in the "Sort & Filter" group on the Ribbon's Home tab:

The Sort & Filter icon group explained

Click here for detailed filter options

Click here to sort data in ascending order

Click here to filter using data in the currently-selected cell

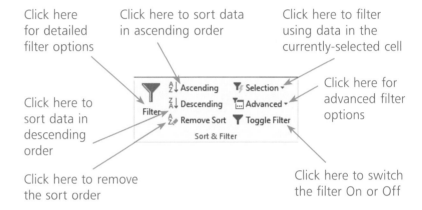

Click here to sort data in descending order

Click here for advanced filter options

Click here to remove the sort order

Click here to switch the filter On or Off

Don't forget

Advanced filters operate in much the same way as the Access **Queries** that are demonstrated in Chapter 6.

94

Filtering by selection

The simplest method of filtering data is to filter by selection. This restricts the number of records seen on screen according to simple criteria. For example, you could apply a filter to a Table of books so that Access will only display the records of books by a particular author:

1 Click the cell containing the data you want to filter

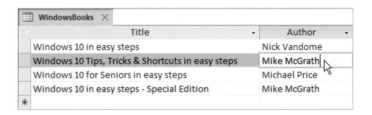

WindowsBooks	
Title	Author
Windows 10 in easy steps	Nick Vandome
Windows 10 Tips, Tricks & Shortcuts in easy steps	Mike McGrath
Windows 10 for Seniors in easy steps	Michael Price
Windows 10 in easy steps - Special Edition	Mike McGrath

2 Next, click the **Selection** icon in the "Sort & Filter" group

3 Now, click a filtering option from the filter menu that appears

4 See that when the filter is applied the only records displayed in Table are those by the selected author, in this case

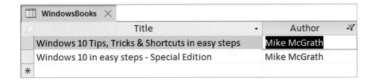

Applying a detailed filter

You can also restrict the records on screen using multiple data values in a detailed filter. You may, for example, want to see only records displayed in the Table of books by two particular authors:

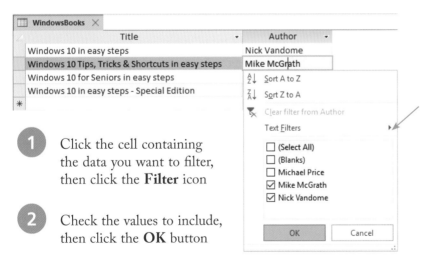

1 Click the cell containing the data you want to filter, then click the **Filter** icon

2 Check the values to include, then click the **OK** button

Hot tip

Click the arrow button beside the **Text Filter** menu item to see all of its filter options, such as "Contains" and "Does Not Contain".

Totaling fields

Access provides a useful Totals function that allows you to sum the values in a field, count the number of records, or find the average value. The function can even perform statistical operations more commonly associated with Excel – for example, finding the standard deviation or variance of the values in a column:

1 Click the **Totals** icon in the "Records" group on the Ribbon's **Home** tab – to see a "Total" row appear below the Table

Title	Price
Windows 10 in easy steps	$14.99
Windows 10 Tips, Tricks & Shortcuts in easy steps	$14.99
Windows 10 for Seniors in easy steps	$14.99
Windows 10 in easy steps - Special Edition	$24.99
*	$0.00
Total	

2 Select a field by clicking a cell in the "Total" row – to see an arrow button appear in the selected cell

3 Click the arrow button to open a drop-down menu of function options

Total
None
Sum
Average
Count
Maximum
Minimum
Standard Deviation
Variance

4 Select the desired function to see the result appear in the selected cell – for example, choose **Sum** to total the values

Title	Price
Windows 10 in easy steps	$14.99
Windows 10 Tips, Tricks & Shortcuts in easy steps	$14.99
Windows 10 for Seniors in easy steps	$14.99
Windows 10 in easy steps - Special Edition	$24.99
*	$0.00
Total	$69.96

Hot tip

You can click the **Totals** icon to toggle the visibility of the "Total" row, and the calculated value will be retained.

Checking spelling

Not only is it possible to check the spelling in a field, you can also choose a specific dictionary to check it against. Spell-checking data can be a good and a bad thing. It is most useful when checking Long Text data, such as that in a Description field, rather than a Short Text field that could, for example, contain a surname. Spell-checkers take great exception to names that they aren't familiar with, and often offer a range of entirely unsuitable alternatives. Unfortunately, unless you specifically highlight a cell, the spell-checker hunts for mistakes field by field, starting with the first record and working its way down to the last, so be sure to check the data value under scrutiny before taking its advice:

To ensure that you have accurate spellings for your region, check the correct dictionary is in use by the spell-checker.

1. Click the **Spelling** icon in the "Records" group on the Ribbon's **Home** tab

2. Use the "Spelling" dialog to locate misspelled words

Misspelled words appear here

Suggested alternatives to the misspelled word appear here

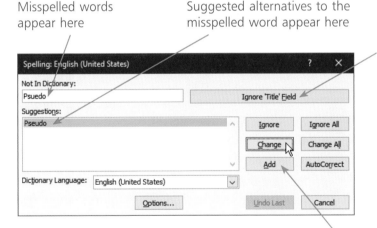

If a field contains data that you know to be correct yet may confuse the spell-checker, click the **Ignore '...' Field** button. The spell-checker will then completely ignore that field.

3. Select a suggested alternative to correct a spelling error, then click the **Change** button to apply your selection

If the spell-checker claims a word is misspelled yet you know it to be correct, click the **Add** button to add the word to the dictionary permanently.

4. Repeatedly change or ignore each further misspelled word until completion

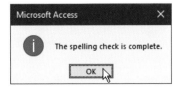

Formatting Tables

The opportunities to format Table data in Access are limited in Datasheet View, but the "Text Formatting" group on the Ribbon's Home tab does provide some useful options:

The Text Formatting icon group explained

Click here to change font

Click here to change font size

Click here to choose list bullets or numbering

Click here to choose list indentation levels

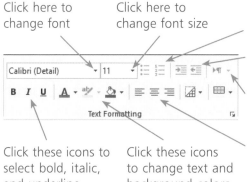

Click here to choose the text direction

Click these icons to select bold, italic, and underline

Click these icons to change text and background colors

Click these icons to select the text alignment

Hot tip

Regardless of the **Alternate Row Color** and **Gridlines** options you choose, the width and height of the records and fields can be altered as usual.

Coloring records

The background color of every other Table record is, by default, a shade darker than the records directly above and below to make the Table easier to read. You can change the darker shade to customize your Tables:

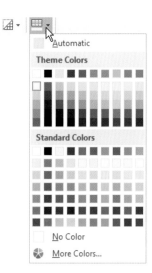

1 Click the **Alternate Row Color** icon

2 Select a color from the drop-down menu that appears

Formatting gridlines

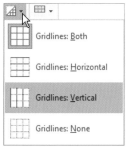

1 Click the **Gridlines** icon

2 Select a gridline style from the drop-down menu that appears

Rich Text Formatting

The ability to apply Rich Text Formatting is available for the Long Text data type, but the application of Rich Text Formatting to a Long Text field can be viewed everywhere that the Long Text field is used – whether it's in a Table, a Form, or a Report:

1 Open a Table in **Design View** to see the data types

Field Name	Data Type
ID	AutoNumber
Title	Short Text
Author	Short Text
Price	Currency
Description	Long Text

2 Select a field of the **Long Text** data type

3 Select the **Text Format** item on the "General" tab in the Field Properties list that appear below the Table

4 Click the arrow button, then select the **Rich Text** option on the drop-down menu

Text Format	Rich Text
Text Align	Plain Text
Append Only	Rich Text

5 Return to **Datasheet View** and select the **Long Text** field

6 Use the icon options in the "Text Formatting" group to modify the text content to your preference

Rich Text Formatting is not available for data types other than the **Long Text** data type.

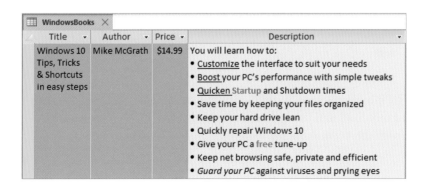

Title	Author	Price	Description
Windows 10 Tips, Tricks & Shortcuts in easy steps	Mike McGrath	$14.99	You will learn how to: • <u>Customize</u> the interface to suit your needs • <u>Boost</u> your PC's performance with simple tweaks • <u>Quicken</u> Startup and Shutdown times • Save time by keeping your files organized • Keep your hard drive lean • Quickly repair Windows 10 • Give your PC a free tune-up • Keep net browsing safe, private and efficient • *Guard your PC* against viruses and prying eyes

...cont'd

Unhiding fields

Hot tip

Fields can be hidden or unhidden by clicking the **More** icon in the "Records" group on the Home tab and clicking the appropriate option in the drop-down menu.

1 Right-click any field heading

2 Select **Unhide Fields** from the context menu – to open the "Unhide Columns" dialog

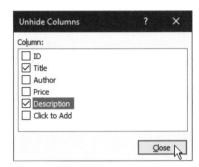

3 Check the boxes of the fields you want to see

4 Click the **Close** button

Freezing fields

Freezing a field ensures that it is always visible within that Table window. This is useful if there is a field that you must constantly refer to during data entry, such as a Name field:

Hot tip

Fields can also be frozen or unfrozen by clicking the **More** icon in the "Records" group on the Home tab and clicking the appropriate option in the drop-down menu.

1 Right-click the field you want to freeze

2 Select **Freeze Fields** from the context menu

To unfreeze a field, simply click the heading of any field and select **Unfreeze All Fields** from the context menu.

6 Making Queries

This chapter describes how to retrieve data, and demonstrates how to specify criteria to seek specific data.

Introducing Queries

When you execute ("run") a Query, you are asking Access to retrieve a set of records from one or more Tables. Selected records are retrieved according to the criteria you provide. For example, you might want to retrieve only records of a single category from the Table of books illustrated below:

MikesBooks			
Title ▾	Price ▾	Category ▾	
C Programming in easy steps	$14.99	Programming	
C# Programming in easy steps	$14.99	Programming	
C++ Programming in easy steps	$14.99	Programming	
Coding for Beginners in easy steps	$14.99	Programming	
Excel VBA in easy steps	$14.99	Programming	
Java in easy steps	$14.99	Programming	
PHP & MySQL in easy steps	$14.99	Web Development	
Python in easy steps	$14.99	Programming	
SQL in easy steps	$14.99	Programming	
Visual Basic in easy steps	$14.99	Programming	
HTML in easy steps	$14.99	Web Development	
CSS in easy steps	$14.99	Web Development	
JavaScript in easy steps	$14.99	Web Development	
Coding for Kids in easy steps	$14.99	Web Development	
Windows 10 in easy steps - Special Edition	$24.99	Operating Systems	
Unix in easy steps	$14.99	Operating Systems	
Windows 10 Tips, Tricks & Shortcuts	$14.99	Operating Systems	
Linux in easy steps	$14.99	Operating Systems	

To retrieve the desired records a "Select" Query can be made, in which you state the category name as the criteria. For example, you might state the "Web Development" category as the criteria:

WebDev Query		
Title ▾	Price ▾	Category ▾
PHP & MySQL in easy steps	$14.99	Web Development
HTML in easy steps	$14.99	Web Development
CSS in easy steps	$14.99	Web Development
JavaScript in easy steps	$14.99	Web Development
Coding for Kids in easy steps	$14.99	Web Development

Although there are many different types of Query, the Select Query is the one most frequently used. Other types of Query include the "Append" Query, which adds new records to an existing Table; the "Delete" Query, which permanently removes records from a Table; and the "Make Table" Query, which makes a new Table using the records it retrieves from other Tables.

Hot tip

A **Query** looks like a Table and, for the most part, behaves like a Table. You can base a Form or Report on a Query, and even use Queries as the source for other Queries.

Employing the Query Wizard

Access provides a "Query Wizard" that allows you to quickly create database Queries. The wizard lets you choose between four different types of Query. The most basic Query is the simple Select Query, which merely lets you nominate fields for selection:

1 Click the Ribbon's **Create** tab to see the "Queries" group

2 Click the **Query Wizard** icon – to open the "New Query" dialog

3 Select the **Simple Query Wizard** option

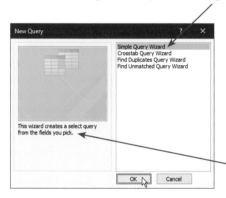

A description appears here of the currently-selected **Query** type.

4 Click the **OK** button – to open the "Simple Query Wizard" dialog

5 Choose a Table or Query to use as the base for your Query from the **Tables/Queries** drop-down menu

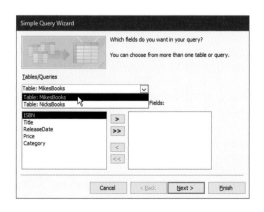

Hot tip

...cont'd

6 Use the arrow buttons in the center of the dialog to select the fields that will be displayed in your Query result

Hot tip

Select the fields in the order you would like them displayed in the results – in columns, arranged left to right.

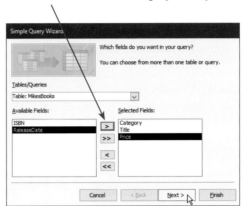

7 Click the **Next** button to continue

If you've included a field that uses a Number-based data type you can have Access calculate the sum, average, minimum, or maximum for that field. To do this, click the **Summary** option button, then click the **Summary Options...** button:

Beware

You are not presented with the options to choose a **Summary** or **Detail** Query unless you have selected one or more fields containing Number-based data.

Check one or more boxes to have the function performed on a field, then click the **OK** button to continue.

...cont'd

Alternatively, if you do not require Summary Options, click the **Detail** option button, then click the **Next** button to continue.

8 Enter an appropriate title to name the Query

9 Click the **Finish** button – to see the Query results displayed in Datasheet View

Category	Title	Sum Of Price
Operating Systems	Linux in easy steps	$14.99
Operating Systems	Unix in easy steps	$14.99
Operating Systems	Windows 10 in easy steps - Special Edition	$24.99
Operating Systems	Windows 10 Tips, Tricks & Shortcuts	$14.99
Programming	C Programming in easy steps	$14.99
Programming	C# Programming in easy steps	$14.99
Programming	C++ Programming in easy steps	$14.99
Programming	Coding for Beginners in easy steps	$14.99
Programming	Excel VBA in easy steps	$14.99
Programming	Java in easy steps	$14.99
Programming	Python in easy steps	$14.99
Programming	SQL in easy steps	$14.99
Programming	Visual Basic in easy steps	$14.99
Web Development	Coding for Kids in easy steps	$14.99
Web Development	CSS in easy steps	$14.99
Web Development	HTML in easy steps	$14.99
Web Development	JavaScript in easy steps	$14.99
Web Development	PHP & MySQL in easy steps	$14.99

You can sort the categories to group the records – right-click on the "Category" field heading and choose **Sort A to Z** from the context menu.

Working with Query Design

Although the Query Wizard lets you choose only those fields that you want to see, it doesn't allow you to specify exacting criteria on which records should be selected. To create more advanced Queries, you will need to use the Query Design View:

1 Click the Ribbon's **Create** tab to see the "Queries" group

2 Click the **Query Design** icon – to open the "Show Table" dialog

The height of the "Show Table" dialog was increased for the modern Access app, in order to list more **Table** and **Query** objects.

3 Select a Table or Query listed in the Show Table dialog, then click the **Add** button – to add your selection to the Query Design window

4 Click the **Close** button to close the dialog

5 Double-click on field names to add them to the bottom Query window

A field can easily be removed by unchecking the **Show** box in the Query window. When you run the Query, the field will not appear.

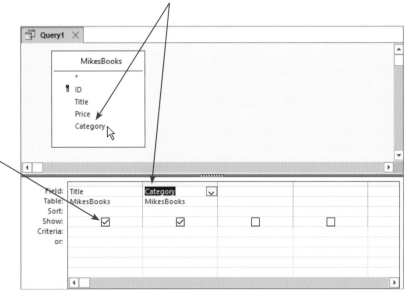

...cont'd

6 Click the **Run** icon in the "Results" group on the Ribbon's **Design** tab – to see the Query results displayed in Datasheet View

Title	Category
C Programming in easy steps	Programming
C# Programming in easy steps	Programming
C++ Programming in easy steps	Programming
Coding for Beginners in easy steps	Programming
Excel VBA in easy steps	Programming
Java in easy steps	Programming
PHP & MySQL in easy steps	Web Development
Python in easy steps	Programming
SQL in easy steps	Programming
Visual Basic in easy steps	Programming
HTML in easy steps	Web Development
CSS in easy steps	Web Development
JavaScript in easy steps	Web Development
Coding for Kids in easy steps	Web Development
Windows 10 in easy steps - Special Edition	Operating Systems
Unix in easy steps	Operating Systems
Windows 10 Tips, Tricks & Shortcuts	Operating Systems
Linux in easy steps	Operating Systems

7 Click the **Save** button on the Quick Access Toolbar – to open the "Save As" dialog

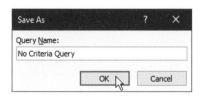

8 Enter an appropriate name, then click the **OK** button to save your Query

Hot tip

You can limit the number of records to be retrieved by setting the **Return** value in the "Query Setup" group on the Design tab.

Don't forget

Saved Queries get added to the **Navigation Pane** and can be opened, executed, or modified whenever you want.

Hot tip

You can also save a Query by clicking the **File** button, then clicking the **Save** option.

Adding criteria to a Query

The most powerful feature of a Query is its ability to select only those records that satisfy a particular condition. For example, you might only want to view all the "Web Development" books in the previous example on page 107. To select records that satisfy this criteria, the category can be specified in the Query Design window:

1 Create a **Query** by following steps 1-5 on page 106

2 Click a cell on the **Criteria** row of the Category column:

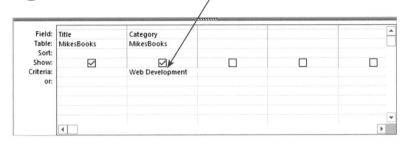

Make sure you save the **Query** if this is an operation you want to carry out in the future.

3 Enter the criteria you want the Query to satisfy – in this case, type "Web Development"

4 Click the **Run** icon in the "Results" group on the Ribbon's **Design** tab – to see the Query results displayed in Datasheet View

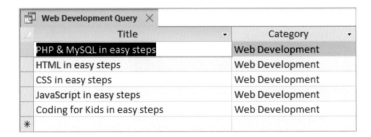

To retrieve all records where there is no value stored within a particular field, type **IS NULL** into the criteria field of the Query design window.

5 Click the **Save** button on the Quick Access Toolbar, then save the Query with an appropriate name

Querying multiple Tables

Queries can include fields drawn from a mixture of Tables. It is also possible to specify criteria for more than one field in order to refine your Query further. For example, you may only want to see the "Programming" books sold online on Christmas Day:

1 Create a **Query** by following the steps on page 106, adding as many Tables as are necessary

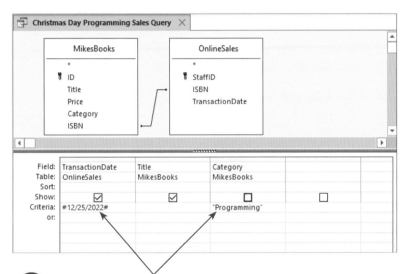

Note that the ISBN key identifies the book in both Tables shown here.

2 Specify the criteria you want to use in your Query

3 Click the **Run** icon in the "Results" group on the Ribbon's **Design** tab – to see the Query results displayed in Datasheet View

Christmas Day Programming Sales Query	
TransactionDate ▾	Title ▾
25-Dec-22	C# Programming in easy steps
25-Dec-22	Java in easy steps
25-Dec-22	SQL in easy steps
25-Dec-22	Java in easy steps
25-Dec-22	SQL in easy steps

Stating criteria for numbers

A good understanding of how to specify criteria is key to creating an effective Query. The kind of criteria in a Query depends on the data type of the fields to which you want to apply the criteria.

Criteria for Number data types

The = "operator" is used to specify a value criteria, to find all records that exactly equal a given value. For example, you might want to find only records where a "Price" field contains $24.99.

The < less-than and > greater-than operators find all records where a value is greater than or less than a given value. For example, you might want to find all records in a Table where a "Price" field contains a value less than $20.00.

The < less-than and > greater-than operators can be combined with the = operator to include values that are exactly equal. For example, you might want to find all records in a Table where a "Price" field contains a value less than $14.99 or is exactly $14.99.

The < less-than and > greater-than operators can also be combined with the **Or** logical operator to exclude a range of values by performing two conditional tests. For example, you might want to retrieve all records in a Table where a "Price" field contains a value below $10.00 or above $20.00.

Conversely, you can specify a range of values to include by using the **Between** and **And** operators. For example, you might want to retrieve all records in a Table where a "Price" field contains a value between $10.00 and $20.00.

Hot tip

The part of the number following the decimal point can, optionally, be omitted if there are no cents. For example, **20.00** can be **20**.

110

Specifying criteria for text

The Query criteria for number-based data types are designed to be specific in the values that are returned by a Query that uses them. Query criteria for text-based data types are designed to retrieve more general results. This is to overcome the complexity of natural language and the problems that occur when a word entered into a Table as a value has been misspelled. For example, to identify only sales staff, you might want to find all the records in a "Staff" Table where a "Position" field contains the word "sales". You can use the **Like** operator followed by a text string:

Notice how the word "sales" has an * (asterisk) placed before and after it. The asterisk is known as the wildcard operator. In the example above, it tells Access that anything before the word "sales" automatically satisfies the Query criteria and that everything after it also satisfies the criteria. This is important because it means you can look for text strings that form part of a field's value rather than the whole. The wildcard operator is useful if you only know part of a value and want to retrieve all the values that contain that part. For example, suppose you only know the first two letters of a staff member's surname and want to search a Table for the names of all staff whose surname begins with those two first letters. You can use the wildcard and **Like** operators again:

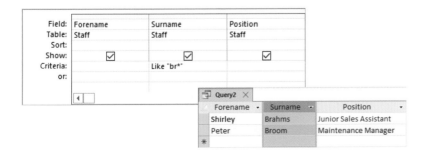

The text criteria is not case-sensitive – notice here how the criteria "*sales*" finds the capitalized text "Sales".

A text string is simply a series of characters enclosed within quote marks.

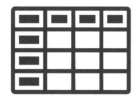

Creating a Make Table Query

A "Make Table Query" is an action Query that, when run, stores its results in a new Table. A Make Table Query is most useful for copying specific records that you want to isolate. For example, you might want to have a separate Table that only contains the titles of books of one specific category:

1 Create a **Query** following steps 1-5 on page 106

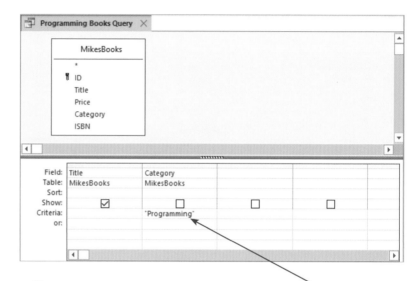

Notice that the "Make Table" dialog also allows you to choose whether to create the new Table in the current database or in another database.

2 Enter any **Criteria** you want to use in the Query; for example "Programming" in a Category field

3 Click the **Make Table** icon in the "Query Type" group on the **Design** tab

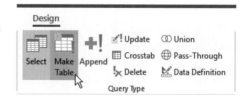

4 Type a new Table name in the "Make Table" dialog

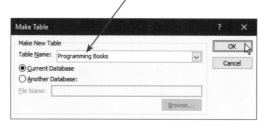

5 Click the **OK** button to close the "Make Table" dialog – see that nothing appears to happen

6 Click the **Run** icon in the "Results" group on the Ribbon's **Design** tab

7 Click the **Yes** button on the warning dialog if you are certain that you now want to run the **Make Table** action Query

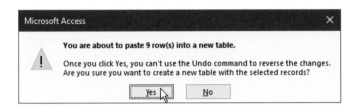

8 The newly-created Table appears in the **Navigation Pane**, and can be opened and used like any other Table

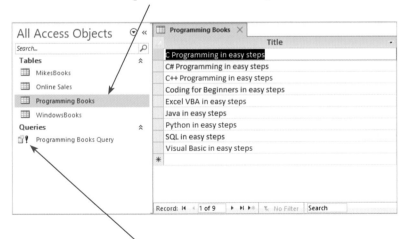

Subsequently running a **Make Table** Query will recreate the original Table and will delete the Table created on the previous run.

9 The action Query also appears in the **Navigation Pane**, and can be run again to recreate the Table if required

Creating an Append Query

An "Append Query" is an action Query that adds the selected records to another Table. For example, you may want to add book titles by another author to a Table of books on a specific category:

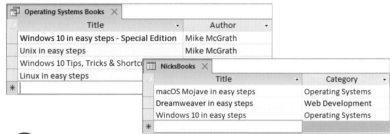

Beware

The effects of running an **Append** Query are permanent and cannot be undone.

Hot tip

Be sure to save the **Append** Query if it is something you will use often.

1 Create a **Query** following steps 1-5 on page 106

2 Enter any **Criteria** you want to use in the Query; for example "Operating Systems" in a Category field

3 Click the **Append** icon in the "Query Type" group on the **Design** tab

4 Choose a Table in which to append the Query results, then click the **OK** button

5 Click the **Run** icon in the "Results" group on the Ribbon's **Design** tab

6 Click the **Yes** button on the warning dialog if you are certain that you want to append the new rows

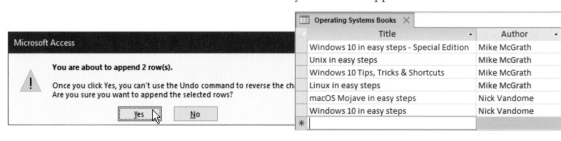

Creating an Update Query

An "Update Query" is an action Query that modifies records that already exist in a Table. For example, you may want to reduce the price of books in a Table during a special promotion period:

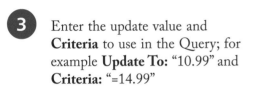

MikesBooks	
Title	Price
C Programming in easy steps	$14.99
C# Programming in easy steps	$14.99
C++ Programming in easy steps	$14.99
Coding for Beginners in easy steps	$14.99
Excel VBA in easy steps	$14.99

1 Create a **Query** following steps 1-5 on page 106

2 Click the **Update** icon in the "Query Type" group on the **Design** tab

Append Update

3 Enter the update value and **Criteria** to use in the Query; for example **Update To:** "10.99" and **Criteria:** "=14.99"

Field:	Price
Table:	MikesBooks
Update To:	10.99
Criteria:	=14.99
or:	

4 Click the **Run** icon in the "Results" group on the Ribbon's **Design** tab

View Run
Results

5 Click the **Yes** button on the warning dialog if you are certain that you want to update the records

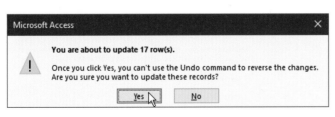

Microsoft Access ✕

⚠ **You are about to update 17 row(s).**
Once you click Yes, you can't use the Undo command to reverse the changes. Are you sure you want to update these records?

[Yes] [No]

MikesBooks	
Title	Price
C Programming in easy steps	$10.99
C# Programming in easy steps	$10.99
C++ Programming in easy steps	$10.99
Coding for Beginners in easy steps	$10.99
Excel VBA in easy steps	$10.99

If you do not specify any criteria, the entire field will be updated to the value specified in the **Update To:** box.

115

Creating a Delete Query

A "Delete Query" is an action Query that removes records from a Table based on the criteria you specify. For example, you may want to remove a book title on release of a new edition:

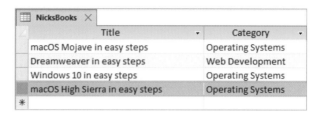

A **Delete** Query permanently removes data from a Table. Only use it if you are certain that the records it affects can be deleted.

1 Create a **Query** following steps 1-5 on page 106

2 Click the **Delete** icon in the "Query Type" group on the **Design** tab

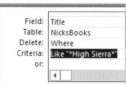

3 Enter the **Criteria** to use in the Query; for example, use the **Like** operator to identify Title text

Field:	Title
Table:	NicksBooks
Delete:	Where
Criteria:	Like "*High Sierra*"
or:	

4 Click the **Run** icon in the "Results" group on the Ribbon's **Design** tab

5 Click the **Yes** button on the warning dialog if you are certain that you want to delete the record

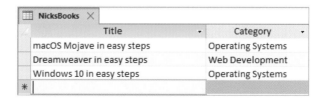

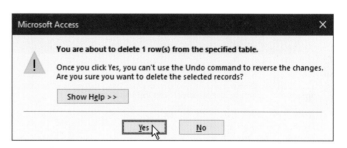

7 Coding Queries

This chapter demonstrates the basics of the SQL programming language that can be used to code your own Queries to retrieve data.

Introducing SQL

Structured Query Language (SQL – pronounced "sequel") is a programming language used exclusively with a Relational Database Management System (RDBMS), such as Access. You can write code in SQL to modify data and create Tables, but SQL is most frequently used to make **SELECT** Queries to retrieve data:

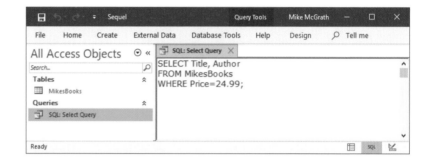

You can adjust the font in the SQL window by navigating through **File**, **Options**, **Object Designers**, **Query design** in Access.

Access uses a dialect of **SQL** that does differ from the standard version in places. Search the Help files for more information.

Why write code?

Given that Access is specifically designed to help users create databases without writing a line of code, you might be wondering why anyone would want to use SQL. One advantage SQL offers is that it can be used with Visual Basic for Applications (VBA) – Access's native programming language. SQL also allows you to create sophisticated Queries very quickly. Once you become familiar with SQL, it's quicker to type out a few lines of code for a **SELECT** Query than to use the graphical Query Design feature.

A brief history of SQL

SQL was first conceived as a standard programming language for Relational Database Management Systems at a time when many competing proprietary languages were in use by different software vendors. Once a business had bought and implemented a database management system from one vendor, they found it hard to migrate their existing database to a system from another vendor. By adopting SQL as the standard database language, software companies found it easier to tempt customers away from their existing RDBMS, and customers were able to take advantage of cheaper or more efficient systems without too much disruption. A standard language also made it easier and faster for software engineers and programmers to implement their database designs.

SQL is a single language, but it comprises three subsets that each provide statements specific to an area of database management:

Data Control Language (DCL)

The statements of this subset allow database administrators to configure security access. For example, they are used to create new users or restrict what a user can do in a database. Access does not, however, support the use of the Data Control Language subset.

Data Definition Language (DDL)

The statements in this subset can be used to create and alter the structure of a database. For example, they are used to create, delete, or add fields in a Table:

When you run an **SQL** query you may see an error message: "Query must have at least one destination field". To avoid this, always save each SQL query in Design View. Alternatively, click **File**, **Options**, **Current Database** and uncheck the **Track name Autocorrect info** item.

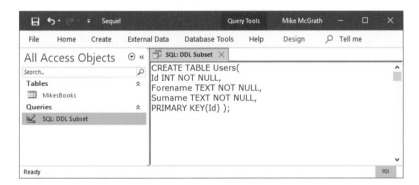

Data Manipulation Language (DML)

The statements in this subset can be used to add, modify, retrieve, or remove data. For example, to make **SELECT** Queries:

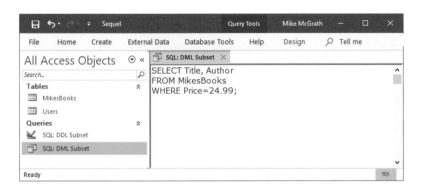

You can discover much more about the Structured Query Language from the companion book in this series, entitled **SQL in easy steps**.

Exploring the SQL window

There are a few different ways to open the SQL window. First, you must open a Query (this can be either an existing Query or a Query that you are in the process of designing), then use any of the following techniques:

- Click the **View** icon in the "Views" group on the Ribbon's **Home** tab, then select the **SQL View** option.

120

- Click the **Data Definition** icon in the "Query Type" group on the Ribbon's **Design** tab.

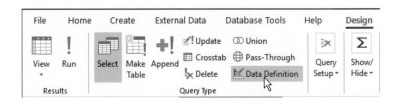

- Click the **SQL** button at the foot of the main Access window.

- Right-click the tab of a Query window, then select **SQL View** from the context menu.

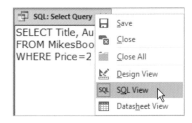

Using the SELECT clause

The SQL Select Query begins with the **SELECT** "clause" (keyword) and is used to specify the fields that are to be displayed when the Query is run. The **SELECT** Query must, like all SQL Queries, end with a **;** semicolon operator.

The most basic **SELECT** Query consists of the **SELECT** clause followed by a comma-separated list of field names to retrieve, then a **FROM** clause followed by the name of the Table to be queried:

When a **SELECT** Query draws its data from more than one Table, it is necessary to distinguish fields with the name of the Table they are selected from. This is achieved by "dot-suffixing" the field name after the Table name – using the "." period operator:

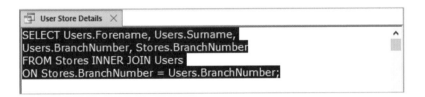

Sometimes, a **SELECT** Query can return results containing so many duplicate values that it can be difficult to interpret the results. For example, suppose you want to see the range of prices of the books within a Table? Running a simple **SELECT** Query to retrieve the Price field from the Table would result in a lot of duplicated prices, because a value from the Price field would be retrieved from every record contained in the Table. This can be avoided by adding a **DISTINCT** clause, to return only unique results:

To run an SQL Query you need to click the Run icon, as usual.

Use the * wildcard character to select all fields in a Table with **SELECT ***. When selecting fields from more than one Table, also specify the Table name, such as **SELECT Users.***.

Each **SELECT** Query must contain a **SELECT** clause and a **FROM** clause.

Using the WHERE clause

The SQL **WHERE** clause specifies the rows to be displayed when the Query is run according to a given condition. The condition could be a comparison of values using mathematical operators, or a logical comparison, or a combination of both. For example,

you might want to retrieve records from this "Users" Table by comparing salary values mathematically.

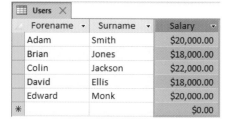

Users		
Forename ▾	Surname ▾	Salary ▾
Adam	Smith	$20,000.00
Brian	Jones	$18,000.00
Colin	Jackson	$22,000.00
David	Ellis	$18,000.00
Edward	Monk	$20,000.00
*		$0.00

The SQL Query shown below uses the **WHERE** clause to select all the records where the salary value is $20,000 or higher:

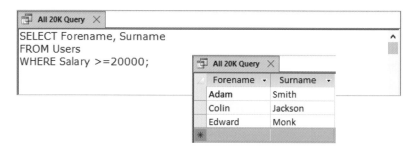

```
All 20K Query  ✕
SELECT Forename, Surname
FROM Users
WHERE Salary >=20000;
```

All 20K Query ✕	
Forename ▾	Surname ▾
Adam	Smith
Colin	Jackson
Edward	Monk
*	

You might then want to be more specific, retrieving records from the "Users" Table by comparing salary values mathematically and by comparing surname values logically.

The SQL Query shown below uses the **WHERE** clause to select all the records where the salary value is $20,000 or higher **AND** where the surname is **NOT** "Monk":

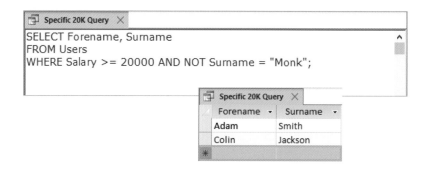

```
Specific 20K Query  ✕
SELECT Forename, Surname
FROM Users
WHERE Salary >= 20000 AND NOT Surname = "Monk";
```

Specific 20K Query ✕	
Forename ▾	Surname ▾
Adam	Smith
Colin	Jackson
*	

Don't forget

Removing **NOT** from the example to the right would make the Query retrieve only records where the salary value is $20,000 or higher, and where the surname is indeed "Monk".

Employing SQL functions

SQL Queries can use aggregate functions such as **COUNT()** and **SUM()** in the same manner they can be used in graphical Queries. To use an aggregate function in SQL you need to specify it after the **SELECT** clause, and include a field name in the parentheses. For example, you might use the **COUNT()** function to find out how many online book sales were made on the date 12/25/2022 by counting the number of entries in an ISBN field:

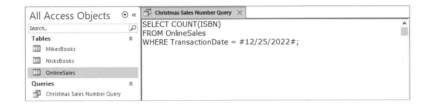

The result shows that a total of five books were sold on that date.

The table below lists the most frequently-used SQL functions, together with a brief description:

Function:	Description:	Example:
SUM()	Sums the values stored in a field	SELECT SUM(*FieldName*) FROM *TableName*
AVG()	Averages the values stored in a field	SELECT AVG(*FieldName*) FROM *TableName*
COUNT()	Counts the number of records in a field that have a value	SELECT COUNT(*FieldName*) FROM *TableName*
MAX()	Finds the highest number in a field	SELECT MAX(*FieldName*) FROM *TableName*
MIN()	Finds the lowest number in a field	SELECT MIN(*FieldName*) FROM *TableName*

Beware

The **COUNT()** function only counts records that have a value in a field, even if that value is zero. To count every record in a Table, use the * wildcard operator in place of the field name, with **COUNT(*)**.

Combining UNION Queries

A SQL **UNION** Query combines the records retrieved by two **SELECT** Queries, from two independent Tables, in one united result. The **UNION** clause is simply added before the second **SELECT** clause. It is, however, important to recognize that each **SELECT** Query must have the same number of fields for output, and they must be in the same order. You might, for example, wish to combine the titles of books from two authors into one result:

A **UNION** Query can only be created in SQL code – it cannot be created graphically. This alone is a great reason to learn how to code your own SQL Queries.

124

1 Click the **Query Design** icon in the "Queries" group on the Ribbon's **Create** tab

2 Close the "Show Table" dialog without adding any Tables

3 Click the **Union** icon in the "Query Type" group on the Ribbon's **Design** tab

4 Type a **SELECT** Query for two fields you want to include from a Table, but exclude one category of book

5 Add a second **SELECT** Query, preceded by a **UNION** clause, for two fields you want to include from another Table

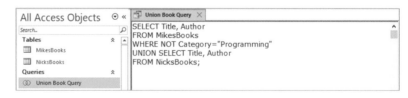

```
SELECT Title, Author
FROM MikesBooks
WHERE NOT Category="Programming"
UNION SELECT Title, Author
FROM NicksBooks;
```

The result combines nine titles by the first author with three titles by the second author.

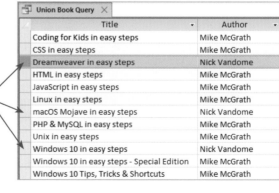

(8) Producing Forms

This chapter demonstrates how to produce user-friendly Forms for easy data entry.

Designing a Form

An Access "Form" is simply a window in which users can enter information into your database. It is a graphical interface between your users and the database you have created. Forms make data entry quicker and easier, and improve the overall user experience.

Why not enter data directly into a Table?

Studies have shown that a well-designed user interface has a positive, beneficial effect on the people who use it. A well-designed Form looks inviting, makes efficient use of the screen space available, and asks only for the specific information required to complete a given transaction.

Access Tables that contain many fields and records may seem daunting to the average user. Updating values in such large Tables might appear confusing to the user, and may possibly lead to errors.

Designing the perfect Form

When designing a Form to be attractive to users, to support all their needs (and yours) it may help to consider these guidelines:

- Make the look and feel of the Form consistent – provide a standard way for users to interact with your Form.

- Use words and familiar terms on the Form – if your database describes widget products, then refer to them on your Form as "widgets" rather than "products".

- Keep the Form clear and uncluttered – do not add unnecessary controls or information onto your Form.

- Thoroughly test the Form – ensure that all controls on your Form perform exactly as expected.

- Build the Form around the tasks that the users of your database will want to carry out – try to anticipate every possible requirement of your Form's users.

An Access Form is used to collect information just as a paper form can be used to collect information, but the Access Form has the advantage of a direct connection to a database.

A badly-designed **Form** will not appeal to users, and will induce user errors.

Form controls

In order to allow user interaction, each Form must provide interactive "control" components such as text boxes and buttons. A control is an object that is designed to perform a particular function, such as taking input from a user or presenting a choice. Every control has a list of properties that dictate the way it looks and behaves. For example, changing a Label control's Font property will change the way the text displayed on it will look.

Controls can be divided into three different varieties:

- **Unbound control** – an unbound control is not linked to a field but is used to merely display information or to support user interaction with the Form itself. For example, Label controls that display text to simply provide instruction.

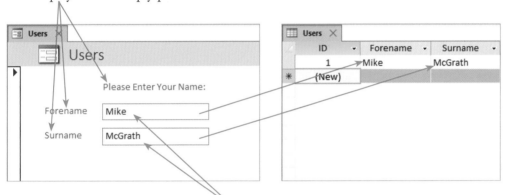

- **Bound control** – a bound control is linked directly to a field in a Table or Query. By changing the value in a bound control, the user also changes the value in the linked field. For example, Text Box controls change text in the fields to which they link.

- **Calculated control** – a calculated control displays a value that is the result of a mathematical expression assigned to its Control Source property. For example, a Text Box control that subtracts a percentage from the value in another field and then displays the result.

Special Offer:	
Regular Price	$14.99
20% Off Price	$11.99

Entering data via a Form

Access automatically provides a navigation bar at the bottom of every Form that makes it easy for the user to navigate through the database Table records:

Click here to move to the **First record**

Current record

Click here to move to the **Last record**

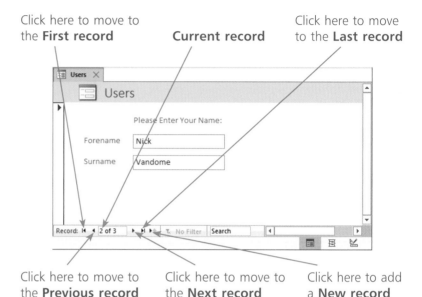

Click here to move to the **Previous record**

Click here to move to the **Next record**

Click here to add a **New record**

Hot tip

If you know the number in the sequence at which the record you want to view or edit appears, you can enter it into the **Current record** field and press Return.

The sequence of records is dictated by the order of the records in the underlying Table or Query upon which the Form is based. The record at the top of a Table will be the first one to be displayed, and the record at the bottom of the Table will be the last.

Adding a new record

The "New record" button on the navigation bar can be used to add new (blank) records to the Table, or the Ribbon can be used:

1 Click the **Home** tab on the Ribbon

2 Click the **New** icon in the Ribbon's "Records" group

Editing data in a Form

1 Click the text field of the value you want to edit

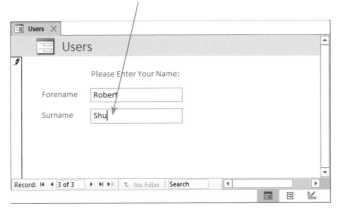

The changes you make to a field will take effect the moment you press the **Tab** key to move into another field.

2 Amend the data, then press the Tab key to move to the next field

You can also press **Shift** + **Tab** to move to the previous field.

Deleting a record

1 Navigate to the record you want to delete

2 Click the Ribbon's **Home** tab to see the "Records" group

3 Click the down arrow to the right of the **Delete** icon to open a drop-down menu

4 Click the **Delete Record** option

Deleting a record is irreversible – be sure you really want to delete the record!

5 Access now displays a warning dialog – click the **Yes** button to delete the record and to close the dialog

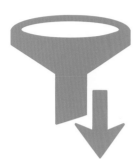

Filtering Form data

You may want to restrict the number of records a Form can access according to some criteria. For example, you might want to see only books that are not in paperback format:

Filtering by selection

1 Select the **Text Box** that contains the criteria you want to use as the filter

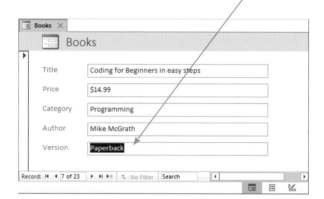

2 Click the **Home** tab on the Ribbon

3 Click the **Selection** icon in the Ribbon's "Sort & Filter" group, then choose the most appropriate filter option

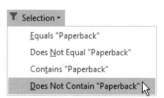

Notice that a **Filtered** button appears on the navigation bar when a filter has been applied. You can click this button to toggle the filter between On and Off.

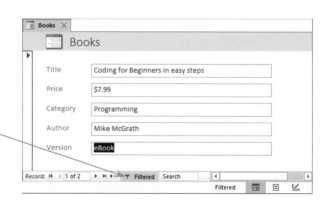

...cont'd

Applying a detailed filter

It's sometimes more useful to filter multiple values rather than limiting the filter to just a single value. For example, you might want to see only books of two specific prices:

1 Select the **Text Box** that contains the criteria you want to use as the filter

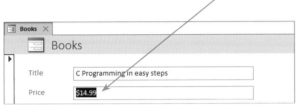

2 Click the **Home** tab on the Ribbon, then click the **Filter** icon in the "Sort & Filter" group

3 Select the criteria for the filter from the menu that appears below the selected Text Box

4 Click the **OK** button to apply the filter, and see the number of records change accordingly

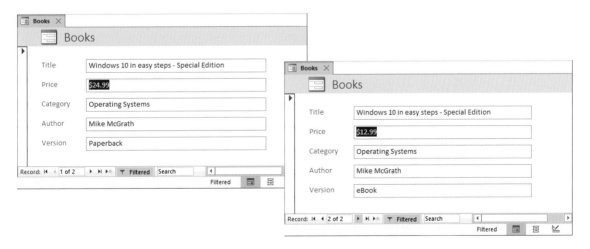

Employing the Form Wizard

Access provides a "Form Wizard" that allows you to produce an attractive data entry Form quickly and easily:

1 Click the **Create** tab on the Ribbon

2 Click the **Form Wizard** icon in the "Forms" group

3 Click the arrow button in the **Tables/Queries** box to open a drop-down menu

You can choose as many or as few fields to appear on the Form as you like – it does not affect the original **Table**.

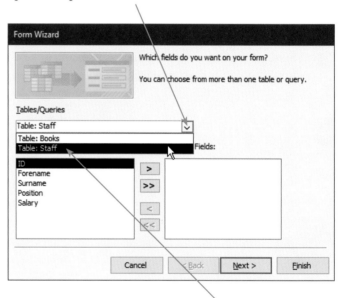

4 From the drop-down menu, choose the **Table** or **Query** upon which the Form should be based

5 Click the arrow buttons to select the fields that you want to appear on the **Form**

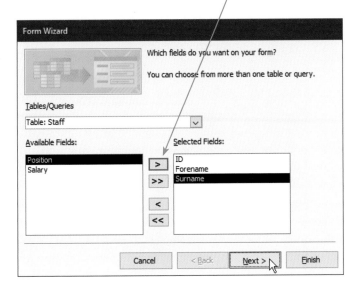

You can use the double-arrow buttons to select or deselect all fields with just one click.

6 Click the **Next** button to continue

7 Select an option button to choose a layout for the Form, then click the **Next** button to continue

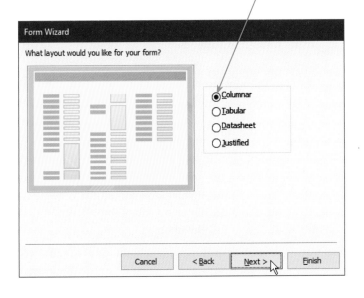

The **Columnar** and **Justified** layouts display a single record on the Form, whereas the **Tabular** and **Datasheet** layouts display multiple records on the Form. Label and Text Box controls on a **Columnar** Form are "anchored" – so can be moved and resized as a group.

...cont'd

8 Type a title for your **Form** here

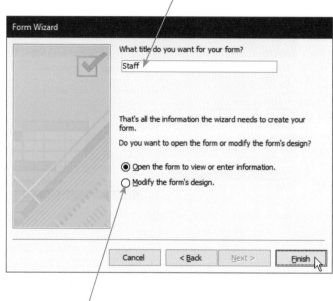

Fine-tuning the layout in **Design View** is described in Chapter 9.

9 Select this option button if you want to open the Form in **Design View** to fine-tune its design

10 Click the **Finish** button – to see Access open the Form in **Form View** ready for you to use

Each new Form created by the **Form Wizard** gets automatically saved and added to the Navigation Pane.

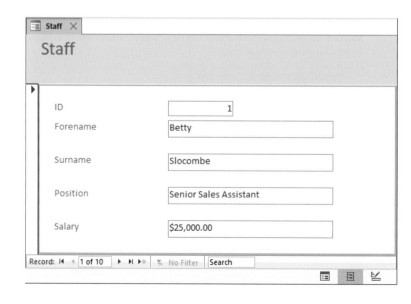

Providing a Simple Form

You can have Access provide a "Simple Form" in just a few clicks
– without even using the Form Wizard:

1 In the **Navigation Pane**, select a
Table or Query upon which the
Form should be based

2 Click the **Create** tab, then choose the **Form** icon in the
Ribbon's "Forms" group

3 See Access generate a Form in **Layout View**, where you
can make simple layout modifications if desired

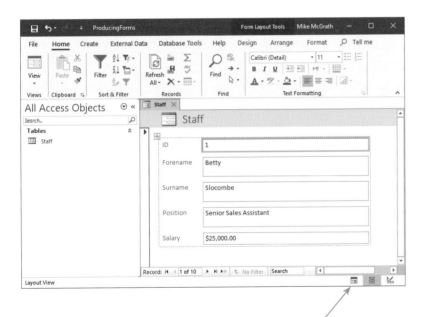

4 To switch to **Form View** for data entry, click the button
on the Status Bar, or select **View**, **Form View** from the
"Views" group on the Ribbon's **Design** tab

Hot tip

Click the **View** icon in
the "Views" group on
the Ribbon's **Design**
tab to find options to
view a Form in **Form
View** (for data entry),
Layout View (for simple
modification), and
Design View (for fine-
tuning the design).

Beware

Unlike with the **Form
Wizard**, each new Form
created by clicking the
Form icon does not get
automatically saved or
added to the Navigation
Pane – you need to save
these Forms manually by
clicking the **Save** icon on
the Quick Access Toolbar.

Offering a Split Form

A "Split Form" combines the easy data entry of Form View with the versatility of a Table in Datasheet View. Split Forms are extremely useful when working with large Tables or Queries that contain a lot of entries or many fields. Users can quickly find the record they need to amend using the Datasheet part of the Split Form, and use the Form part of the Split Form to modify it:

You can only modify the design of the **Form** part of a Split Form – you cannot modify the **Datasheet** part.

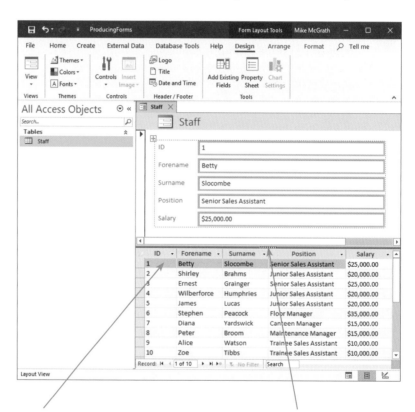

Click a record in the **Datasheet** part to display it in the **Form** part

Drag the splitter bar to resize the **Datasheet** part and **Form** part

A Split Form is much more than a novel means of data entry, as it has specific properties that can be used to fine-tune the design. For example, the position of the Datasheet part of the Split Form can be changed to suit your requirements.

Creating a Split Form

1 In the **Navigation Pane**, select a Table or Query upon which the Form should be based

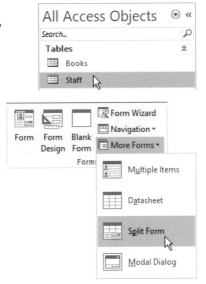

2 Click the Ribbon's **Create** tab

3 Click **More Forms** in the "Forms" group

4 Choose the **Split Form** option on the drop-down menu

Unlike with the **Form Wizard**, each new Form created by clicking the **More Forms**, **Split Form** option does not get automatically saved or added to the Navigation Pane – you need to save these Forms manually by clicking the **Save** icon on the Quick Access Toolbar.

Fine-tuning Split Forms

1 Click **View**, **Design View** in the "Views" group on the Ribbon's **Home** tab – to switch to Design View

2 Press the **F4** key (or **Fn** + **F4**) to open the **Property Sheet**

3 Click the arrow button in the "Selection type" box, then choose **Form** from the drop-down menu

4 Scroll down the list to see the **Split Form** properties and their current values

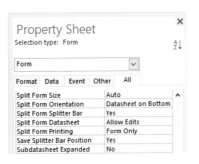

All the Split Form specific properties can be accessed by clicking the **Format** tab on the Property Sheet.

...cont'd

Changing the position of the Datasheet

The default position of the Datasheet part of a Split Form is below the Form part. It can be moved above the Form part if preferred by changing the Split Form Orientation property value to "Datasheet on Top":

Split Form Orientation	Datasheet on Bottom
Split Form Splitter Bar	Datasheet on Top
Split Form Datasheet	Datasheet on Bottom
Split Form Printing	Datasheet on Left
Save Splitter Bar Position	Datasheet on Right
Subdatasheet Expanded	No

Not all Split Form specific properties can be altered in **Layout View** – use **Design View** instead.

Removing the Splitter Bar

After carefully designing your Split Form, you might want to disable the users' ability to modify its appearance using the Splitter Bar. The bar can be completely removed from the Form by changing the **Split Form Splitter Bar** property value to "No":

Split Form Orientation	Datasheet on Bottom
Split Form Splitter Bar	Yes
Split Form Datasheet	Yes
Split Form Printing	No
Save Splitter Bar Position	Yes
Subdatasheet Expanded	No

Setting Datasheet properties

To prevent users from making mistakes when using the Datasheet, you might want to disable the users' ability to modify its data. Users will still be able to locate a record using the Datasheet part but must use the Form part when entering or modifying data. The Datasheet can be safeguarded by changing the **Split Form Datasheet** property value to "Read Only":

Split Form Orientation	Datasheet on Bottom
Split Form Splitter Bar	Yes
Split Form Datasheet	Allow Edits
Split Form Printing	Allow Edits
Save Splitter Bar Position	Read Only
Subdatasheet Expanded	No

Presenting Multiple Items

A "Multiple Items Form" displays many records on screen at the same time in a tabular, user-friendly format:

1 In the **Navigation Pane**, select a Table or Query upon which the Form should be based

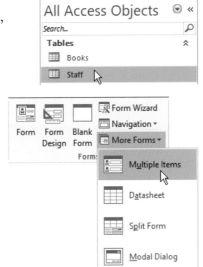

2 Click the Ribbon's **Create** tab

3 Click **More Forms** in the "Forms" group

4 Choose the **Multiple Items** option on the drop-down menu

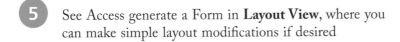

5 See Access generate a Form in **Layout View**, where you can make simple layout modifications if desired

Unlike with the **Form Wizard**, each new Form created by clicking the **More Forms, Multiple Items** option does not get automatically saved or added to the Navigation Pane – you need to save these Forms manually by clicking the **Save** icon on the Quick Access Toolbar.

139

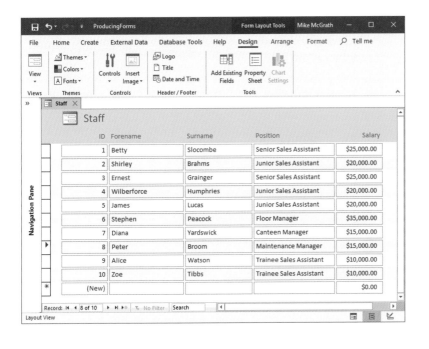

As with any **Form**, the design can be modified to suit your requirements.

Finding a record

Finding a specific record with a Form that displays only one record at a time is made easy with the "Find and Replace" facility:

1 Click the **Text Box** of the field you want to search

2 Click the **Find** icon in the "Find" group on the Ribbon's **Home** tab – to open the "Find and Replace" dialog

3 Enter a value to search for into the **Find What** box

4 Choose whether to search for data that fully or partially matches the value you are searching for

5 Choose whether you just want to search that specific field or the entire **Form**

6 Click the **Find Next** button to see the search results

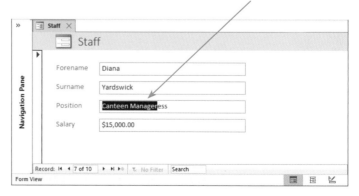

9 Enhancing Forms

This chapter demonstrates how to add Form controls and Macro code for greater Form functionality.

Working with Design View

The "Design View" of Table and Query database objects enables you to easily modify those objects to suit your data requirements. Similarly, the Design View of Form objects enables you to enhance Forms to suit your functionality requirements:

1 Click the **Create** tab on the Ribbon

2 Click the **Form Design** icon in the "Forms" group

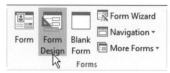

3 See Access generate a new blank Form displayed in **Design View** – ready for customization

Use the **Themes** drop-down menu to choose the Form's appearance.

Use the ruler to adjust the position of Form controls, such as a **Label** or **Text Box**

Use the **Property Sheet** to change the look and behavior of the Form and Form controls

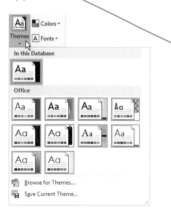

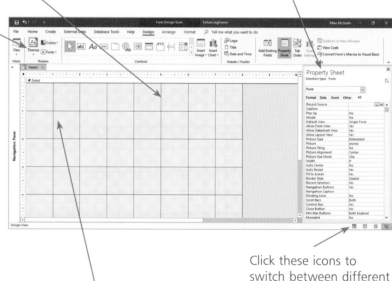

Hot tip

If the **Property Sheet** does not automatically appear, press the **F4** key (or **Fn + F4**) to open it.

Place controls onto the **Detail** section to create a Form design

Click these icons to switch between different **Views** of the Form

Employing the Field List

The Access "Field List" enables you to easily add Text Box and Label controls to a Form that are instantly bound (linked) to an existing field in the database:

1 Open a Form in **Design View**

2 Click the **Add Existing Fields** icon in the "Tools" group on the Ribbon's **Design** tab – to open the **Field List**

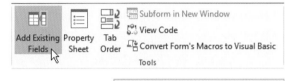

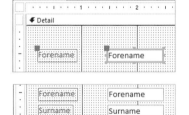

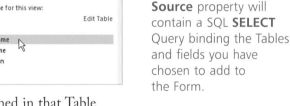

Hot tip

In the **Property Sheet**, the Form's **Record Source** property will contain a SQL **SELECT** Query binding the Tables and fields you have chosen to add to the Form.

3 Click the expand/collapse button to the left of any Table name – to see the fields contained in that Table

4 Double-click on a field you want to add to the Form – to see a bound **Label** and **Text Box** control appear in the **Detail** section

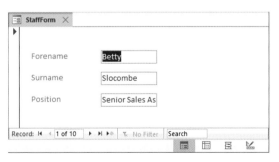

5 Repeat the previous step to add more fields

6 Click the button at the bottom of the Access window to switch to **Form View** – to see data retrieved from the bound fields

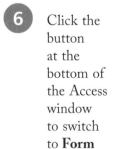

Don't forget

Notice that the default size of the Text Box may not accommodate the text length of some data. The example overleaf demonstrates how to easily correct this in **Layout View**.

Working with Layout View

Adding controls to design a Form in Design View lets you produce an attractive functional Form with precision, but Design View does not display database field data in the controls – in Design View, a control will merely display the name of the field from which to retrieve data when the Form is active. For example, a Text Box control whose function is to retrieve data from a "Title" field will only display the name "Title" in Design View.

Switching from Design View to "Layout View" lets you quickly review your Form design with database field data displayed in the controls, and allows you to make simple changes to the look and feel of a Form. For example, you might need to extend the size of a Text Box to accommodate the text length of some field data:

Resizing controls in Layout View

1 Click on a control to select it – see its outline turn orange to indicate the control is selected

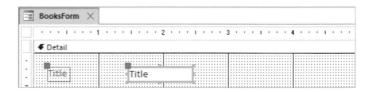

Hot tip

You can also adjust the size of a selected control by changing its **Width** and **Height** values in the Property Sheet.

2 Click the button at the bottom of the Access window to switch to **Layout View**

3 Place the cursor over the orange outline, then hold down the mouse button and drag the control to extend its size

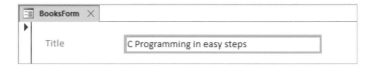

Adding Headers and Footers

When creating a Form, Design View will, by default, automatically display the "Detail" section – to which you can add functional dynamic controls that interact with the database. Other sections, such as a "Header" and "Footer", can be added to a Form – to which you can add static controls that do not interact with the database:

Viewing Headers and Footers

1 Right-click the **Detail** section of a Form

2 Select the type of Header you want to view from the context menu

Build Event...	
▣	Tab Order...
📋	Paste
🎨	Fill/Back Color ▸
▦	Alternate Fill/Back Color ▸
▥	Ruler
▦	Grid
▧	Page Header/Footer
▤	Form Header/Footer
▤	Form Properties
▤	Properties

Hot tip

Icons on this context menu that appear highlighted indicate selected features. For example, click **Ruler** or **Grid** to toggle those features On or Off.

Form Headers and Form Footers
These sections are typically used to display corporate information, such as a company name and logo. Controls placed in the Form's Header and Footer can be seen both on screen and in print:

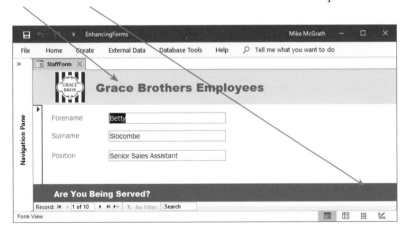

Page Headers and Page Footers
These sections are only visible when you print a Form or Report. This is useful for information you may not want to appear on the screen but want to include when printed. For example, company contact information included for a Form that is used to create invoices that are printed out then mailed to clients.

Adding controls to a Form

Form controls perform different functions and have different properties, but the procedure for adding them to a Form is the same for each control:

1 Open a Form in **Design View**

2 Click an icon in the "Controls" group on the Ribbon's **Design** tab – for example, click the **Label** icon

3 Place the cursor at the position where you want the top left-hand corner of the control to be

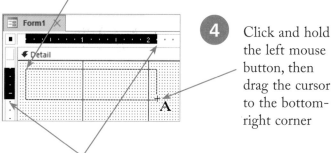

4 Click and hold the left mouse button, then drag the cursor to the bottom-right corner

5 Watch the rulers to help set the control size

6 Release the left mouse button to create the control – see a blinking cursor appear on the control

7 Type some text onto the control to complete the Label

Hot tip

The black bars on the rulers indicate the size the control would be if you released the mouse button at that point. Accurate sizing is particularly important for uniformity when adding more than one control of the same type, such as a row of **Button** controls.

Fine-tuning Form controls

Resizing a control

1 Click a control to select it – see the control gain an orange border with eight "grab handles"

2 Click on a grab handle, then drag in the desired direction

3 Release the mouse button to resize the control

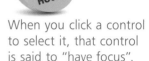

When you click a control to select it, that control is said to "have focus".

Moving a control

1 Click a control to select it

2 Move the cursor to the top of the orange border – see the cursor gain "arrowheads"

3 Click and hold the mouse button, then drag the control to the desired location

4 Release the mouse button to move the control

Attaching a Label to a control

1 Click a descriptive **Label** control to select it

2 Click the **Cut** icon in the "Clipboard" group on the Ribbon's **Home** tab

You can switch to **Layout View** to check whether a control is big enough to contain the linked data.

3 Click the control you want to attach the **Label** to – for example, click on a **Button** control

4 Click the **Paste** icon in the "Clipboard" group to attach the Label to the Button

Changing control properties

Each control, including the Form itself, has a set of properties. You can change these property values to modify a control for your specific needs. For example, you might want to make the text on a Button control blue, or you might want to change the font of the text on a Label control. The "Property Sheet" can be used in Layout View or Design View to change control properties:

1 Click the **Property Sheet** icon in the "Tools" group on the Ribbon's **Design** tab – to open the Property Sheet

2 Click the arrow button in the "Selection type" box at the top of the Property Sheet – to open a drop-down menu

3 Select the control you want to modify from the menu

4 Click the **All** tab to see all that control's properties

5 Select the property to change by clicking its current value

6 Insert a new value, then hit **Enter** to apply the change

When selected, some value boxes provide option menus and swatches by which to insert a new value, but others do not:

You can also open the Property Sheet by pressing the **F4** key (or **Fn** + **F4**).

Clicking on a control changes the focus of the **Property Sheet** to that control – so you can see and change its properties.

- Simply type a new value into value boxes that provide no option menus – such as the **Width** property.

- If an arrow button is present, click the button to select a new value from an option menu – such as the **Font Size** property.

- If an "..." ellipsis button is present, click the button to select a new value from a swatch – such as the **Back Color** property.

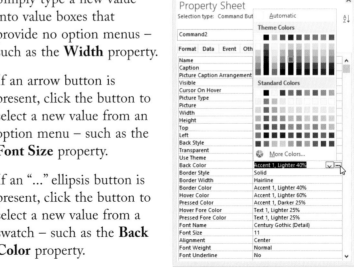

Creating Calculated controls

A "Calculated control" gets its value from an expression entered into its Control Source property. This can be found in the Property Sheet on the Data tab and on the All tab. An expression might be used to calculate a 20% reduction off a "Price" field and display the reduced value in a Text Box control:

1 Open a Form with "Price" field data in **Design View**

2 Add a **Text Box** control to the Form, and select it

3 Press **F4** (or **Fn** + **F4**) to open the Property Sheet

4 Click the **All** tab on the Property Sheet

5 Click the **Control Source** property's value box, then enter the expression to calculate a 20% reduction
= [Price] - [Price] * 0.2

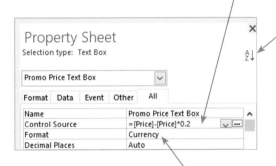

6 Click the **Format** property's value box, then change the value to "Currency"

7 Switch to **Form View** to see the Text Box control display the reduced value in Currency format

The Property Sheet lists dozens of properties. To make it easier to find a property by name, modern Access provides a button to sort the properties into alphabetical order.

Do not use a Text Box control that has been added to a Form from the Field List as a **Calculated** control. These must get their values from an existing database field, not a calculated expression.

Adjusting the Tab Order

Pressing the Tab key in Datasheet View shifts focus from cell to cell of a Table. Similarly, pressing the Tab key in Form View shifts focus from control to control on a Form.

Access automatically sets the "Tab Order" to match the order in which the controls were added to the Form, but you can easily specify a different Tab Order to match the user's requirements:

1 Click the **Tab Order** icon in the "Tools" group on the Ribbon's **Design** tab – to open the "Tab Order" dialog displaying the tab order in top-to-bottom sequence

2 Click here to select a section of the **Form**

3 Click here and hold down the mouse button to select a Form control name

Hot tip

You can click the **Auto Order** button to restore the original Tab Order.

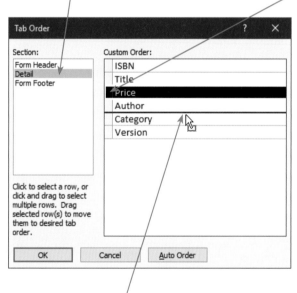

4 Drag the selected control name to a new order position

5 Release the mouse button to change the **Tab Order**

6 Repeat steps 3-5 until you are satisfied with the order

7 Click the **OK** button to apply the changes

Producing a Tabbed Form

The "Tab Control" makes it easy to organize information from different sources into a logical order within a single Form control. The Access Ribbon is a good example of the way tabs can be used to organize information and objects within a single Form control. A Form with a Tab Control is more formally referred to as a "Multi-Page Form" – each tab representing one page:

Adding a Tab Control to a Form

1 Open a Form in **Design View**

2 Click the **Tab Control** icon in the "Controls" group on the Ribbon's **Design** tab

3 Click the mouse at the point on the Form where you want the top-left corner of the **Tab Control** to be placed

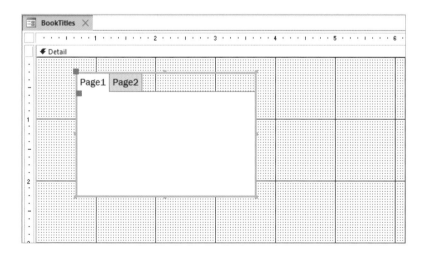

Hot tip

You can have more than one row of tabs on a Tab Control by setting its **Multi Row** property value to **Yes** in the Property Sheet.

4 See a **Tab Control** appear, providing two tabs by default

...cont'd

Adding more Tabs

1 Right-click on any tab of a **Tab Control**

2 Select **Insert Page** from the context menu

3 See a new tab get added to the **Tab Control**

Organizing Tabs

1 Right-click on any tab of a **Tab Control**

2 Select **Page Order...** from the context menu

3 Click the page you want to move to select it

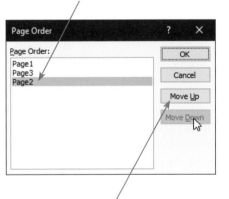

Hot tip

Right-click on a tab you want to remove, then select **Delete Page** from the context menu.

4 Click the **Move Up** or **Move Down** button to organize the order of the tabs

5 Click the **OK** button to apply the change

Adding controls to a page

A Tab Control allows you to place controls on each page to separate field data for greater clarity. For example, you might want to separate data from a Table of books so the user can browse through titles, yet easily find other information on a particular title by selecting other tab pages:

1 Click the **Tab Control** page where you want to add a control to display field data

2 Click the **Add Existing Fields** icon in the "Tools" group on the Ribbon's **Design** tab – to open the **Field List**

3 Drag an item from the Field List onto the page – to add **Label** and **Text Box** controls to display its data

4 Delete the Label, then select the page and assign a label value to the **Name** property on the **Property Sheet**

You can refer to the **Property Sheet** to ensure you are placing a control on the desired page.

5 Repeat steps 1-4 for each page of the **Tab Control**, then open **Form View** to see the separated field data

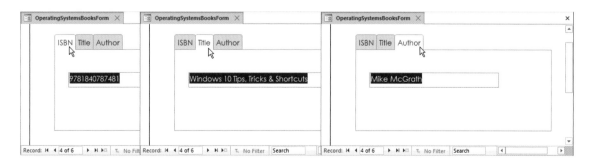

Using Command Buttons

The "Command Button" control is very versatile as it can be used to open database objects, switch views, or support a variety of data entry tasks. For example, you might want to provide a button on a Form which the user can push to move between records:

1 Open a Form in **Design View**

2 Click the **Button** icon in the "Controls" group on the Ribbon's **Design** tab

3 Click the Form to add a **Command Button** control

4 See Access open a "Command Button Wizard" – choose one of the offered **Categories** of functionality

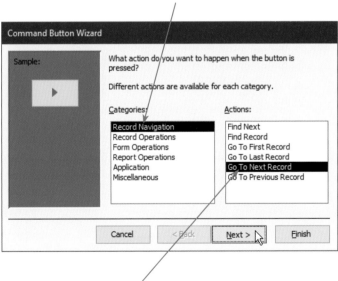

5 Select one of the **Actions** available for that Category

6 Click the **Next** button to continue

Hot tip

The Command Button Wizard offers great choices, but you may prefer to build your own functionality in VBA code. Click the **Cancel** button to close the Command Button Wizard, then right-click the **Button** control and choose the **Build Event** option on the context menu. Select **Code Builder** to open the VBA Editor, where you can write your event-handler functionality.

7 Click an option button to specify whether the **Command Button** control should display Text or a Picture

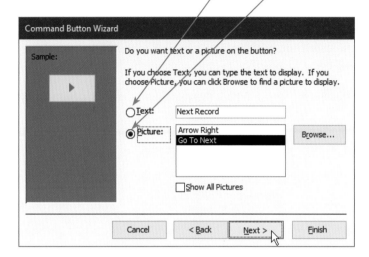

Hot tip

Access provides a default **Picture** for each **Action**, but you can design your own picture then use the **Browse** button to display it on the Command Button control.

8 Click the **Next** button to continue, then type a name for the **Command Button** control

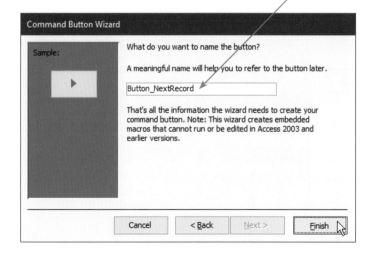

Hot tip

When naming controls, it is recommended you begin with the control type followed by a meaningful name – this readily identifies the control for VBA code.

9 Click the **Finish** button to close the Wizard, then open **Form View** to try the Command Button functionality

Displaying a Modal Dialog

The term "Modal" may be unfamiliar to you, but you will have encountered a Modal Dialog before. It's simply a warning dialog that demands a "yes" or "no" response before allowing the user to continue. A Modal Dialog prohibits access to any app until the user has pressed a button on the dialog. This is useful to safeguard the user from accidental errors. For example, you might want to ask the user whether they're certain they want to close a database:

1 Click the **More Forms** icon in the "Forms" group on the Ribbon's **Create** tab

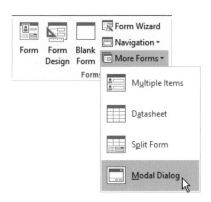

Hot tip

You can convert an existing Form into a Modal Dialog by changing its **Modal** property value to **Yes** in the Property Sheet.

2 Click the **Modal Dialog** option on the drop-down menu

3 See Access open a Modal Dialog in **Design View** – complete with an **OK** button and a **Cancel** button at the bottom right of the Form

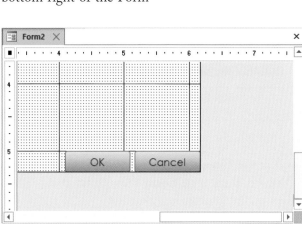
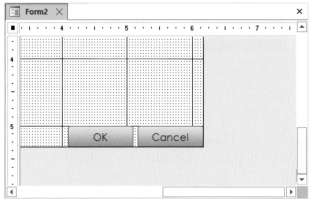

4 Click the **Label** icon in the "Controls" group on the Ribbon's **Design** tab

5 Move the cursor to the point on the Form where you want the top-left corner of the **Label** control to be

6 Hold down the mouse button and drag the cursor to the bottom right to create a rectangle

7 Release the mouse button to create the **Label** control

8 Type questioning text into the **Label** control

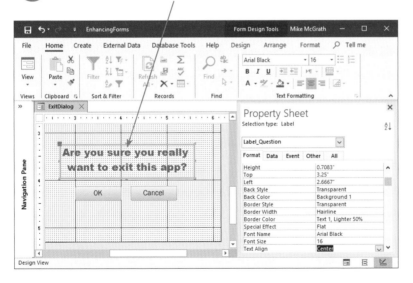

It is good practice to give meaningful names to your **Form** controls.

9 Click the **Property Sheet** icon in the "Tools" group on the Ribbon's **Design** tab – to open the Property Sheet

10 Change the Label's **Text Align** property value to **Center**

...cont'd

11 Click the **OK** Button control – to see its properties in the **Property Sheet**

12 Click the **On Click** property's value box – to see option buttons appear there

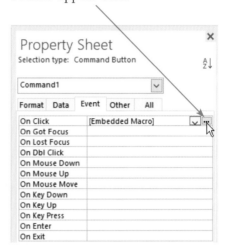

If you open a Modal Dialog in **Form View** you cannot switch to **Design View**. To open a Modal Dialog in **Design View**, right-click it in the Navigation Pane and select Design View from the context menu.

13 Click the **"..."** ellipsis button – to open a **Macro Builder** window

14 Click the **Add New Action** arrow button

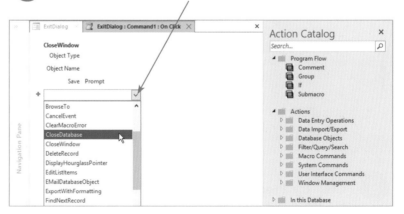

15 Select the **CloseDatabase** action on the drop-down menu

...cont'd

16 Click the **Close** icon in the "Close" group on the Ribbon's **Macro Tools Design** tab – to close the Macro Builder window

17 Click the **Yes** button on the warning dialog that now appears – to save the selected Macro action

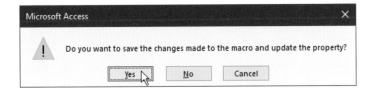

The **Macro Tools Design** tab is only visible when a **Macro Builder** window is open, and its "Close" group is only visible when a Macro is open in **Macro Builder**.

18 Open the Modal Dialog in **Form View**, then click the **Cancel** button – to merely dismiss the dialog

19 Open the Modal Dialog in **Form View** once more, then click the **OK** button – to instantly close the database

159

Executing Macros

A "Macro" is a set of actions that perform particular functions when executed. They are typically used in association with Forms, where they execute in response to an "event" triggered by the user. For example, when the user pushes a Command Button control:

Macros are miniature programs that can automate mundane tasks by combining actions sequentially. This **Macro** example performs three actions – open a Form, go to the first empty record (ready to enter new data), then display a warning message.

1 Click the **Macro** icon in the "Macros & Code" group on the Ribbon's **Create** tab – to open a **Macro Builder** window

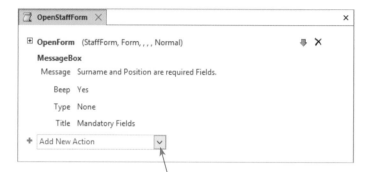

Macros are powerful, and can damage or delete the data in your database if you use them carelessly. Be sure you fully understand the consequences of executing an action before you include it in a Macro.

2 Click the **Add New Action** arrow button, and select actions to perform from the drop-down menu

3 Click the **Save** button on the Quick Access Toolbar, then click the **Run** icon in the "Tools" group on the Ribbon's **Macro Tools Design** tab – to perform the selected actions

10 Supplying Reports

This chapter describes how to create Reports to summarize database information, and demonstrates how to print labels from records.

Exploring the Report Wizard

An Access "Report" allows you to view, format, and summarize your database information. For example, you may want to supply a summary Report of sales across different regions, or supply a simple Report of phone numbers for all your contacts. The quickest way to produce an attractive, professional-quality Report is to use the "Report Wizard":

1 Click the **Report Wizard** icon in the "Reports" group on the Ribbon's **Create** tab – to open the Report Wizard

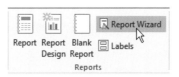

Hot tip

You can include fields from more than one **Table** or **Query** in the Report Wizard.

2 Select the **Table** or **Query** you want to base the Report on from the drop-down menu

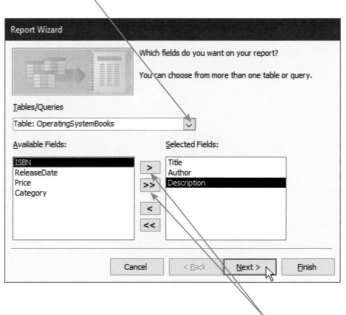

Hot tip

Use the single arrow buttons to move individual items between the Available Fields and Selected Fields, or use the double arrow buttons to move all items with a single click.

3 Select the fields to include in the **Report** by clicking the top two arrow buttons

4 Click the **Next** button to continue

5 Use the arrow buttons to specify grouping levels

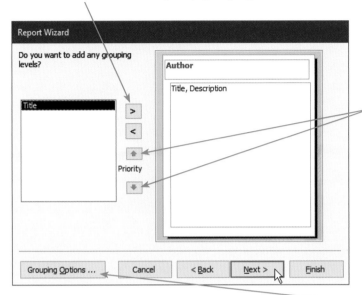

Hot tip

You can use the **Priority** buttons to organize the groups if you have more than one grouping level.

Hot tip

You can also set grouping intervals if you click the **Grouping Options...** button.

6 Click the **Next** button to continue

7 Specify the sort order for the Report by selecting fields from the drop-down menus, then click the **Next** button

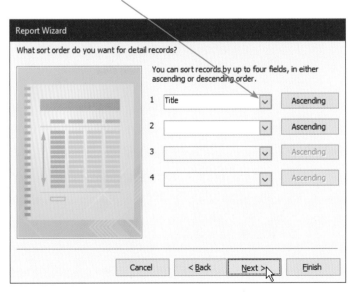

...cont'd

The Report Wizard provides a visual indication in this window of how the selected **Layout** will look.

8 Choose the Report layout by selecting an option button

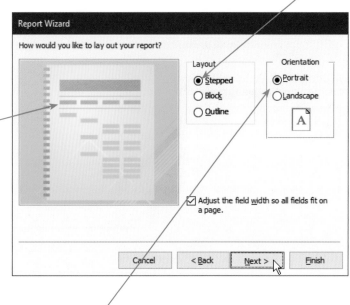

Choose **Landscape** orientation if the Report includes many fields.

9 Choose the Report orientation by selecting an option button, then click the **Next** button to continue

10 Type a title for the Report here

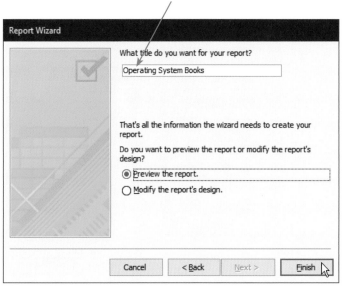

...cont'd

11 Choose to "Preview the report" (or "Modify the report's design" in Design View) by selecting an option button

12 Click the **Finish** button to generate the Report

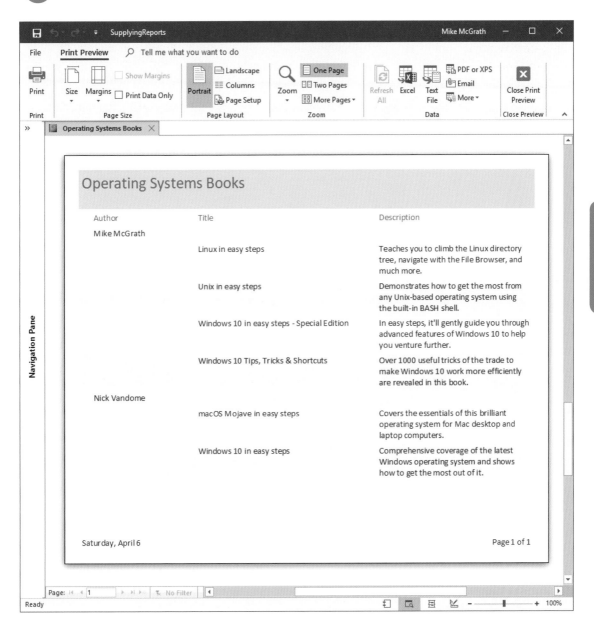

Providing a Simple Report

Access can create an attractive "Simple Report" from scratch with just a couple of clicks:

1 Select a **Table** or **Query** in the Navigation Pane for which you want to construct a Report

2 Click the **Report** icon in the "Reports" group on the Ribbon's **Create** tab

3 See Access generate a **Simple Report** in Layout View – ready for fine-tuning

Don't forget

Remember to save the generated Report by clicking the **Save** icon on the Quick Access Toolbar or by pressing the **Ctrl + S** keys.

4 To switch between views, click the buttons at the bottom of the Report

Report View   Print Preview   Layout View   Design View

Working with Design View

Creating a Report in Design View gives you the ultimate creative freedom to present your data exactly as you need it. The process of constructing a Report in Design View is pretty much the same as that of creating a Form in Design View (see page 142). All the same controls are at your disposal and you have access to the Property Sheet and Field List, just as in Form Design View. The essential difference is that the end product is intended for the printed page, and for that reason the icon groups in "Report Design" View are specifically geared towards page layout:

Creating a Report in Design View

1 Click the **Report Design** icon in the "Reports" group on the Ribbon's **Create** tab

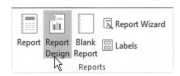

2 See Access generate a new blank Report displayed in **Design View** – ready for customization

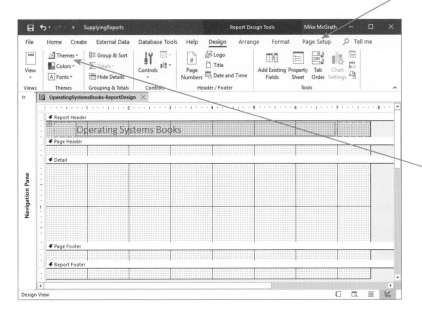

Click the **Page Setup** tab to adjust the page orientation, margins, and columns of the Report.

Use the **Themes** drop-down menu to choose the Report's appearance.

3 Click the **Title** icon in the "Header/Footer" group on the Ribbon's **Design** tab

4 Type a Report title in the **Report Header** section

Adding fields to a Report

When you need to create a Report in a hurry, the Field List is indispensable. By clicking a few field names in the Field List, you can create the essentials of a Report in minutes – giving you time to concentrate on the appearance of the Report so you can present the data in an attractive format:

1 Open a Report in either **Layout View** or **Design View**

You can also open the Field List by pressing the **Alt** + **F8** keys.

2 Click the **Add Existing Fields** icon in the "Tools" group on the Ribbon's **Design** tab – to open the **Fields List**

3 Click the expand/collapse button to the left of any Table name – to see the fields contained in that Table

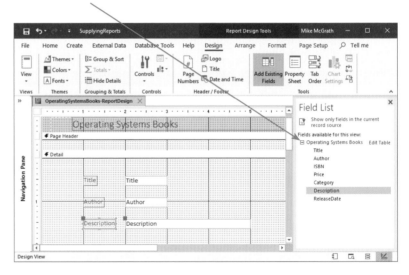

Hot tip

Click an **Edit Table** link in the Field List to open that Table for editing in Datasheet View.

4 Double-click on fields you want to add to the Report – to see bound **Label** and **Text Box** controls appear in the **Detail** section

5 Click the **Reports View** button at the bottom of the Access window to see how the Report looks with data

Adding controls to a Report

The procedure to add a control to a Report is much the same as the procedure to add a control to a Form:

1 Open a Report in **Design View**

2 Click the **Design** tab, then select a control from within the "Controls" icon group

3 Click the point on the Report where you want the top-left corner of the control to be positioned

4 Hold down the mouse button and drag the cursor to the bottom right

5 Release the mouse button to add the control

6 Adjust the control to suit your needs by changing its property values on the **Property Sheet**

Resizing a control on a Report

1 Click a control to select it – see an orange border with eight "grab handles" appear

2 Hold down the mouse button over any grab handle and drag the cursor in your preferred direction

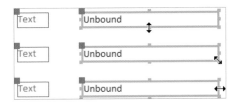

3 Release the mouse button to resize the control

You can open the Property Sheet by pressing the **F4** key (or **Fn** + **F4**).

You can divide the Report into sections by adding **Line** controls from the "Controls" group on the Design tab.

Adding Headers and Footers

Reports can be enhanced by the addition of Header and Footer sections. The type of Header and Footer you choose will depend on whether you want the information they contain to appear only at the beginning of the Report, or on every Page.

1 Open a Report in **Design View**, then right-click on the Report

2 Select **Page Header/Footer** or **Report Header/Footer** from the context menu that appears

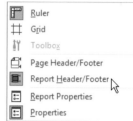

The Report Header
This section will appear only once, at the very beginning of a printed Report, so is best suited for title, logo, and contact details.

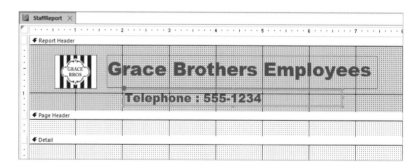

The Page Header
This section will appear at the top of every Page of a printed Report, so is best suited to column-heading labels.

The Page Footer
This section will appear at the bottom of every Page of a printed Report, so is best suited to calculated Page numbering.

The Report Footer
This section will appear only once, at the bottom of the last Page of a printed Report, so is best suited for grand totals of columns.

Sorting and grouping data

Grouping and sorting the data in a Report can help to present the data in a more useful format. For example, you might want to create a Report where book data is grouped by author name, and with the titles of each author's books sorted from A to Z:

1 Open the Report in **Layout View** or **Design View**

2 Click the **Group & Sort** icon in the "Grouping & Totals" group on the Ribbon's **Design** tab

3 See the **Group, Sort, and Total** pane open at the bottom of the main Access window – to display the current grouping and sorting structure of the Report

4 Click the **Add a group** button

5 Select the field you want to use for grouping data from the menu that appears. For example, choose to group on "Author"

6 Now, click the **Add a sort** button

7 Select the field you want to use for sorting data from the menu that appears. For example, choose to sort by "Title"

171

Printing labels

Access provides a "Label Wizard" that is useful for printing data to sticky labels for addressing mail, making visitor passes, creating stickers for client files, etc. The Label Wizard generates a Report, which can be modified like any other Report:

1 Find the **Product number** of your sticky labels on their packaging, and make a note of it

2 Use the Navigation Pane to open the **Table** or **Query** that contains the data for your labels

3 Click the **Labels** icon in the "Reports" group on the Ribbon's **Create** tab – to open the Label Wizard

4 Click the arrow button in the **Filter by manufacturer** box, then select the brand of your sticky labels from the drop-down menu

Beware

It your labels don't print properly, check that you've specified the correct **Unit of Measure** for your labels – many manufacturers use the same **Product number** for their English and Metric labels.

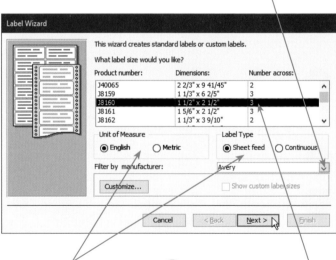

5 Click option buttons to select the **Unit of Measure** and **Label Type** of your sticky labels

6 Scroll through the list, and select the **Product number** that matches your sticky labels

7 Click the **Next** button to continue

8 Click the arrow buttons to open drop-down menus, then choose the **Font** and **Text color** for print on the labels

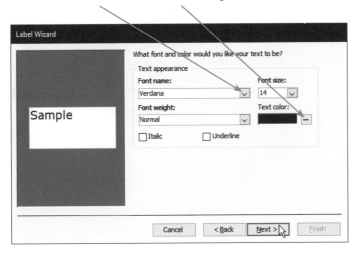

The Preview Pane at the left of the dialog is updated to reflect the **Font** and **Text color** choices you have made.

173

9 Click the **Next** button to continue

10 Click a field to select it, then click the arrow button to add it to the **Prototype label** box

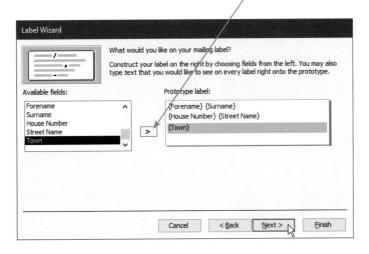

Add a space between each field on the same line and press the Return key to begin a new line. You can also type text into the **Prototype label** box to add a note.

11 Repeat the previous step to complete the **Prototype label**

...cont'd

12 Click the **Next** button to continue, then click the arrow button to choose how you want your sticky labels sorted. For example, sort alphabetically by surname

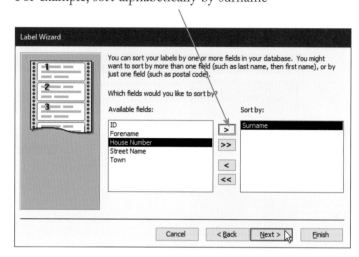

You can make use of the double-arrow buttons to add and remove all the fields in one click.

13 Click the **Next** button, then type a name for the Report and click the **Finish** button to see a Print Preview

Alternatively, you can select the option button to **Modify the label design** to open the Report in **Design View** when you click Finish.

Setting custom label sizes

If your sticky labels have no Product number, you can produce a Report to print them by creating a custom "New Label" size. This requires you to carefully measure the dimensions of the sticky labels and their precise position on the sheet:

1 Use the Navigation Pane to open the **Table** or **Query** that contains the data for your labels

2 Click the **Labels** icon in the "Reports" group on the Ribbon's **Create** tab – to open the **Label Wizard**

3 Click the **Customize** button – to open the "New Label Size" dialog

4 Click the **New** button – to open the "New Label" dialog

5 Enter the sticky label dimensions and their position on the sheet into all boxes on the dialog

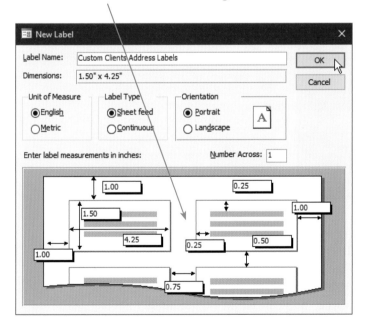

Remember to select the correct **Unit of Measure** and add a **Label Name**.

6 Click the **OK** button to close the "New Label" dialog, then click the **Close** button on the "New Label Size" dialog – to continue on with the Label Wizard as usual

Using Print Preview

The Access "Print Preview" is much more than a means of reviewing a Report before it is sent to the printer. Print Preview allows you to set the margins of a Report, split a Report into two or more columns, and export the Report to other apps.

Switching to Print Preview

There are three ways of switching to the Print Preview view:

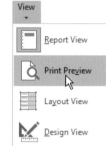

- Click the **View** icon in the "Views" group on the Ribbon's **Home** tab, then select **Print Preview** from the menu.

- Click the **Print Preview** button at the bottom of the Report window (as shown on page 166).

- Click the **File** tab to switch to the Backstage window, then choose the **Print** item on the left and select the **Print Preview** option.

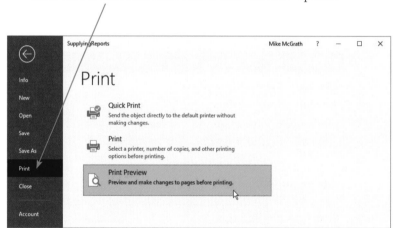

Adjusting Page Layout settings

The "Page Layout" icon group on the **Print Preview** tab contains powerful options to fine-tune your Reports before you print them. For example, click the **Page Setup** icon to open the "Page Setup" dialog, where you can choose **Print Options**, **Page** printer settings, and **Columns** layout.

You must have a Report open before you can view it in Print Preview – the View menu will not contain options for **Report View** and **Print Preview** until you open a Report in Access.

You must have a Report open in **Print Preview** view to see the Print Preview tab.

Printing Reports

When a Report is complete, with all adjustments made to suit
your preferences, Access provides several ways to print the Report:

Print Preview

1 Open a Report in **Print Preview** view

2 Click the **Print** icon in the "Print" group on the **Print Preview** tab – to open the "Print" dialog

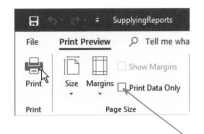

Backstage

1 Open a Report in **Print Preview**, then click the **File** tab

2 Choose the **Print** item on the left, and select the **Print** option – to open the "Print" dialog

Using the Print dialog

Click this arrow button to select a printer from a drop-down menu

Click here to set printer-specific property options

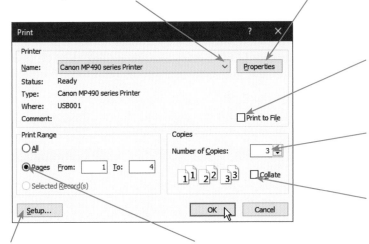

Click here to specify margin sizes and column settings

Click this option button to print a range of pages

Check the **Print Data Only** box if you want to print only data retrieved from the database – text labels will not appear.

Check the **Print to File** box if you want to print out the Report and also save a copy as a Printer File; select the **Number of Copies** you want; and choose whether to **Collate** the pages sequentially if printing more than one copy.

Sending Reports via email

A Report can be exported in a variety of file formats for distribution, and can be distributed by email directly from Access:

1 Select a **Report** you want to email in the Navigation Pane

2 Click the **External Data** tab on the Ribbon

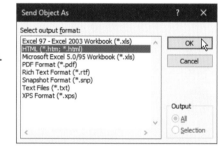

3 Click the **Email** icon in the "Export" group – to open the "Send Object As" dialog

4 Select the type of file you want to export the Report as. For example, choose to export it as an HTML document

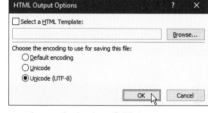

Hot tip

The option to **Select a HTML Template** allows you to nominate an HTML file with which to consolidate the Report – see pages 92-93 for details.

5 Click the **OK** button – to open the "HTML Output Options" dialog

6 Select an encoding type, such as the popular **UTF-8** encoding, then click the **OK** button

7 See the default email client on your system open a new message, with the exported Report already attached

11 Sharing Access

This chapter demonstrates how to secure and share databases with Access.

Protecting with passwords

Sharing data between colleagues is generally a great idea, but it introduces the possibility of confidential, sensitive records stored in your Access database falling into the wrong hands.
To safeguard against this possibility, it is sensible to add password protection to databases that are to be shared:

1 Ensure the database you want to password-protect is completely closed

2 Click the **File** tab to open the Backstage window, then select **Open** from the left menu

3 Click the **Browse...** option, then use the "Open" dialog to navigate to the database you want to password-protect

4 Select the database – but do not open it

5 Click the down arrow to the right of the **Open** button to open a drop-down menu

Hot tip

Use lengthy passwords that are a mixture of numbers and letters, in a mixture of uppercase and lowercase, for better security. Avoid using pet names or family names.

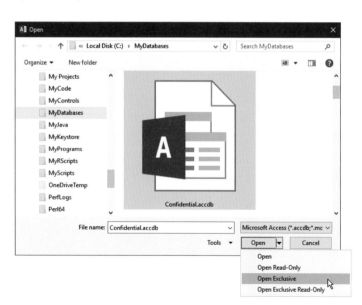

6 Click the **Open Exclusive** option to open the selected database in "Exclusive mode" – so that other users cannot interrupt the task of adding password protection

7 In Access, click the **File** tab to open the Backstage window, then select **Info** from the menu

8 Click the **Encrypt with Password** option

9 Enter your password twice, then click the **OK** button – see a warning dialog appear

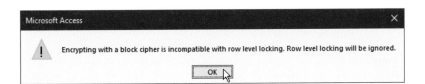

A "block cipher" is encryption applied to the entire block of data, and "row-level locking" prevents other users from accessing a record while it is being updated. The warning dialog is simply explaining that the entire database will be encrypted – not just the record (row).

10 Click the **OK** button to close the warning dialog and to apply the password protection to the database

11 Reopen the database to see you now need to enter the password

Removing password protection

1 Select **Info** in the Backstage window, then click the **Decrypt Database** option

2 Enter your password, then click the **OK** button to remove password protection from the database

A database needs to have been opened in Exclusive mode to set or remove password protection.

Preventing alteration

If a database is to be shared between colleagues, or is to be used by more than one person, it's a good idea to create an ACCDE database. An ACCDE database is similar to a regular ACCDB database except that users cannot alter the design of Forms or Reports, and only compiled VBA code will be included. Creating an ACCDE copy of a regular ACCDB database is a great way of preventing users from accidentally damaging the database:

1 Click the **File** tab to open the Backstage window, then select **Save As** from the left menu

2 Select **Save Database As,** then click the **Make ACCDE** option in the "Advanced" section

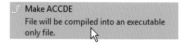

Make ACCDE
File will be compiled into an executable only file.

3 Click the **Save As** button – to open the "Save As" dialog

Save As

4 Navigate to your databases folder, then click the **Save** button – to create an ACCDE copy of your database

Beware

Remember to keep the regular ACCDB version of the database somewhere safe – so you can make changes as the database evolves over time.

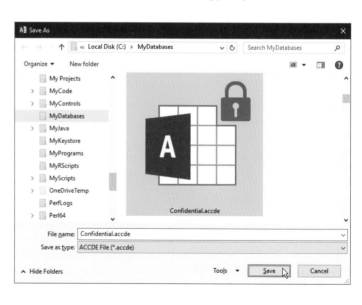

Securing with backups

There are many ways in which data can either be corrupted or lost. Databases could be completely erased by users, either accidentally or maliciously, or an electrical spike could irreparably damage your hard drive. No computer is completely safe, so you should always create regular backups of your data and store them in a safe place. Always store your backups on some form of remote storage, such as a USB drive or an external hard drive:

1 Click the **File** tab to open the Backstage window, then select **Save As** from the left menu

2 Select **Save Database As**, then click the **Back Up Database** option in the "Advanced" section

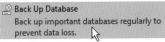

Back Up Database
Back up important databases regularly to prevent data loss.

3 Click the **Save As** button – to open the "Save As" dialog

Save As

4 Navigate to your database's folder, then click the **Save** button – to create a backup copy of your database

183

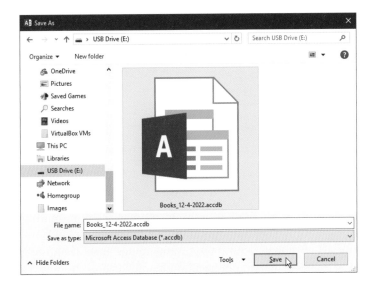

Do not create a backup on the same hard drive used to store your databases – that will not help if the hard drive fails.

Add a date suffix to the database filename so you can easily find the latest backup.

Splitting databases

Splitting a database allows you to separate an Access database into a "Front-end" file containing all the Forms and Queries, and a "Back-end" file containing all the data Tables.

A split database can be used in exactly the same way as any other database, but the Navigation Pane adds arrow icons beside the Table names to denote that they are linked Tables:

1 Open the database you want to split

2 Click the **Database Tools** tab on the Ribbon

3 Click the **Access Database** icon in the "Move Data" group on the Ribbon – to open the "Database Splitter" dialog

Beware

Notice the warning on the "Database Splitter" dialog that the new **Back-end** database will be created without a password – even for password-protected databases.

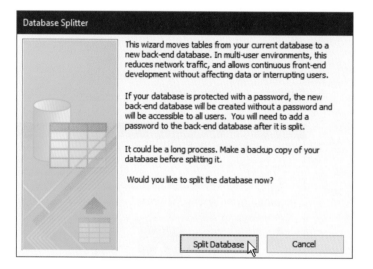

Database Splitter

This wizard moves tables from your current database to a new back-end database. In multi-user environments, this reduces network traffic, and allows continuous front-end development without affecting data or interrupting users.

If your database is protected with a password, the new back-end database will be created without a password and will be accessible to all users. You will need to add a password to the back-end database after it is split.

It could be a long process. Make a backup copy of your database before splitting it.

Would you like to split the database now?

Split Database   Cancel

4 Click the **Split Database** button on the dialog – to open the "Create Back-end Database" dialog

5 Navigate to your databases folder, then click the **Split** button – to create a "Back-end" file containing Tables

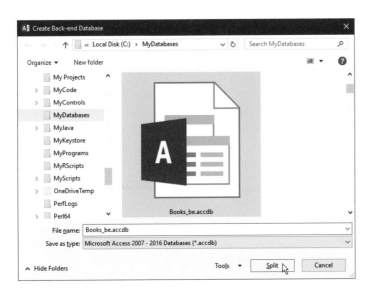

Access automatically suggests a filename that has **_be** (Back-end) appended to the existing filename.

6 See a confirmation dialog appear – click the **OK** button to close the dialog

Updating Back-end Tables

1 Click the **External Data** tab on the Ribbon

2 Click the **Linked Table Manager** icon in the "Import & Link" group – to open the "Linked Table Manager" dialog

The **Linked Table Manager** is a new feature of the modern Access app.

3 Check the Tables to update, then click the **Refresh** button

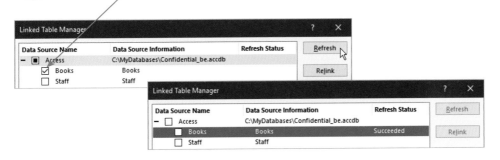

Interacting with SharePoint

"SharePoint Server" is an application server that unifies an organization's web presence, intranet and business documentation. SharePoint Server also integrates with Access. The import and export features of Access allow you to upload data to, and download data from, a SharePoint site. A SharePoint site stores data as lists, which differ according to user needs and permissions. When you upload a Table or Query to a SharePoint site it is converted to a list, and converted to a Table when downloaded.

Importing from or linking to a SharePoint Site

1 Click the **New Data Source** icon in the "Import & Link" group on the Ribbon's **External Data** tab

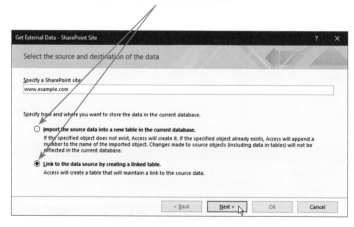

2 Select the **From Online Services** menu item, then choose the **SharePoint List** option – to open the "Get External Data - SharePoint Site" dialog

3 Enter the address of the SharePoint site, then click an option button to specify whether you want to **Import** data from or **Link** to a SharePoint list

When you perform an import operation you can save the import instructions by checking the relevant box in the **Import Wizard**. You can even set an Outlook task to remind you to execute the import instructions.

4 Click the **Next** button, then choose the lists you want to **Import** from or **Link** to, and click the **OK** button

Index

E

F

G

H

I

J

K

L

R

S